全国职业技能英语系列教材

ENGLISH FOR PETROLEUM ENGINEERING

石油工程英语

主 编 郭 凡
副主编 尹海艳 杨会香
编 者 张诗觅 马 鑫

北京大学出版社
PEKING UNIVERSITY PRESS

图书在版编目(CIP)数据

石油工程英语/郭凡主编. —北京：北京大学出版社，2008.9
（全国职业技能英语系列教材）
ISBN 978-7-301-13829-8

Ⅰ. 石… Ⅱ. 郭… Ⅲ. 石油工程－英语－高等学校：技术学校－教材 Ⅳ. H31

中国版本图书馆 CIP 数据核字（2008）第 067923 号

书　　　名：	石油工程英语
著作责任者：	郭　凡　主编
责 任 编 辑：	刘　爽
标 准 书 号：	ISBN 978-7-301-13829-8/H・1992
出 版 发 行：	北京大学出版社
地　　　址：	北京市海淀区成府路 205 号　100871
网　　　址：	http://www.pup.cn
电　　　话：	邮购部 62752015　发行部 62750672　编辑部 62755217　出版部 62754962
电 子 信 箱：	zbing@pup.pku.edu.cn
印　刷　者：	北京大学印刷厂
经　销　者：	新华书店
	787 毫米×1092 毫米　16 开本　9.25 印张　210 千字
	2008 年 9 月第 1 版　2015 年 12 月第 4 次印刷
定　　　价：	28.00 元（配有光盘）

未经许可，不得以任何方式复制或抄袭本书之部分或全部内容。
版权所有，侵权必究
举报电话：(010)62752024　电子信箱：fd@pup.pku.edu.cn

全国职业技能英语系列教材

编委会

顾问

胡壮麟（北京大学）　　　　刘黛琳（中央广播电视大学）

总主编

丁国声（河北外国语职业学院）

编委会名单（以姓氏笔画为序）

丁小莉（山东商业职业学院）
王乃彦（天津对外经济贸易职业学院）
牛　健（中央广播电视大学）
伍忠杰（电子科技大学）
李相敏（河北外国语职业学院）
李恩亮（江苏海事职业技术学院）
张　冰（北京大学出版社）
张九明（开封大学）
张春生（衡水职业技术学院）
陆松岩（江苏城市职业学院）
陈玉华（成都航空职业学院）
林晓琴（重庆电力高等专科学校）
赵　倩（重庆机电职业技术学院）
赵　鹏（北京联合大学）
赵爱萍（浙江水利水电专科学校）
赵翠华（承德民族师范高等专科学校）
胡海青（南京交通职业技术学院）
贾　方（辽宁装备制造职业技术学院）
黄宗英（北京联合大学）
崔秀敏（承德石油高等专科学校）
蒋　磊（河南商业高等专科学校）
程　亚（江西景德镇陶瓷学院）
黎富玉（成都航空职业学院）
潘月洲（南京工业职业技术学院）
Martin Fielko（Cornelsen Press GmbH & Co. KG）

总 序

我国高职高专教育的春天来到了。随着国家对高职高专教育重视程度的加深,职业技能教材体系的建设成为了当务之急。高职高专过去沿用和压缩大学本科教材的时代一去不复返了。

语言学家 Harmer 指出:"如果我们希望学生学到的语言是在真实生活中能够使用的语言,那么在教材编写中接受技能和产出技能的培养也应该像在生活中那样有机地结合在一起。"

教改的关键在教师,教师的关键在教材,教材的关键在理念。我们依据《高职高专教育英语课程教学基本要求》的精神和编者做了大量调查,秉承"实用为主,够用为度,学以致用,触类旁通"的原则,历经两年艰辛,为高职高专学生编写了这套专业技能课和实训课的英语教材。

本套教材的内容贴近工作岗位,突出岗位情景英语,是一套职场英语教材,具有很强的实用性、仿真性、职业性,其特色体现在以下几个方面:

1. 开放性

   本套教材在坚持编写理念、原则及体例的前提下,不断增加新的行业或岗位技能英语分册作为教材的延续。

2. 国际性

   本套教材以国内自编为主,以国外引进为辅,取长补短,浑然一体。目前已从德国引进了某些行业的技能英语教材,还将从德国或他国引进优秀教材经过本土化后奉献给广大师生。

3. 职业性

   本套教材是由高职院校教师与行业专家针对具体工作岗位、情景过程共同设计编写。同时注重与行业资格证书相结合。

4. 任务性

   基于完成某岗位工作任务而需要的英语知识和技能是本套教材的由来与初衷。因此,各分册均以任务型练习为主。

5. 实用性

　　本教材注重基础词汇的复习和专业词汇的补充。适合于在校最后一学期的英语教学，着重培养和训练学生初步具有与其日后职业生涯所必需的英语交际能力。

　　本教材在编写过程中，参考和引用了国内外作者的相关资料，得到了北京大学外语编辑部的倾力奉献，在此，一并向他们表示敬意和感谢。由于本套教材是一种创新和尝试，书中瑕疵必定不少，敬请指正。

丁国声

教育部高职高专英语类专业教学指导委员会委员

河北省高校外语教学研究会副会长

河北外国语职业学院院长

2008年6月

出 版 说 明

  本教材是在《全国职业技能英语系列教材》总主编、教育部高职高专英语教学指导委员会委员、河北外国语学院校长丁国声教授及北京大学出版社外语编辑部张冰主任的主持下,组织全国各地的二十余位英语教学专家讨论编写的,以服务职业培训为原则,将实用性、灵活性的理念融入具体的内容当中的一本技能教材。本教材是北京大学出版社出版的系列职业技能英语教材的一个部分,特点是注重职业仿真环境下工作语言情景的导入,让学生在了解岗位主要流程、工作内容、工作职责、相关知识、文化背景和职业操守的同时,达到能运用英语自如应对涉外工作的目的。

  本书所选的职业岗位是石油工程(管道建设)中的一些涉外岗位,由系统内多年参加海外工程项目的专家,高、中级工程师杨会香、赵海鸿、史小波、高玉桂等同志反复商榷修改,吴春丽、赵亚平、唐江华、吴建中等同志给予了大力协助,在此表示衷心感谢。

  此书的出版将填补本行业的空白,所涉及的内容具有非常强的实用性,可以为参与石油行业涉外工程的高级技术工人提供充分的语言保障,也可作为行业出国施工人员的培训教材。

  由于时间仓促,错误在所难免,恳请广大读者批评指正。

编者
2008.3

CONTENTS

Unit 1 Pipeline Exploration and Design（管网勘探与设计） …………………………… 1

Unit 2 Pipeline Engineering（管道工程） ……………………………………………… 12

Unit 3 Equipment Installation（设备安装） …………………………………………… 23

Unit 4 Anticorrosion Pipeline（管道防腐） …………………………………………… 35

Unit 5 Oil and Gas Transportation（油气集输） ……………………………………… 46

Unit 6 Welding Engineering（焊接工程） ……………………………………………… 58

Unit 7 Engineering Monitoring（工程监理） …………………………………………… 69

Unit 8 HSE（健康、安全、环保） ……………………………………………………… 80

Unit 9 Engineering Maintaining and Repairing（工程维修） ………………………… 94

Unit 10 Station Management（场站管理） …………………………………………… 108

KEY TO QUESTIONS ……………………………………………………………………… 121

Vocabulary ………………………………………………………………………………… 130

Phrases ……………………………………………………………………………………… 135

参考书目 …………………………………………………………………………………… 137

Unit 1

Pipeline Exploration and Design

管网勘探与设计

Look at the following activities involved in pipeline designing. Can you add more?

- review of design process
- document preparation
- feasibility study
- apparatus verification
- responsibility
- process design
- process calculation
- anti-corrosion engineering
- electric design
- cathodic protection
- power supply
- communication equipment operation
- fire-fighting equipment
- supervising control and data acquisition system

Now answer the following questions.

1. Can you sum up the above activities to two categories?
2. If you are a pipeline designer, what do you think is the most important quality in your job?
3. Suppose you are a worker dealing with process calculation, what tasks would you perform? How would you enrich your working experience?

OCABULARY ASSISTANT

feasibility study 可行性研究　　data acquisition 数据采集
cathodic protection 阴极保护　　anticorrosion 防腐

Unit 1
Pipeline Exploration and Design

AIMS
- Preparation for Designing
- Execution of Designing

Part One Word Power

Find the definition in Column B which matches the word or expression in Column A.

A	B
1. pipeline flow diagram	A means and apparatus of underground communicating
2. field survey	B natural products which manufacturing processes turn into another
3. mapping	C a pipeline running from the storage tanks in the field to a major pipeline
4. seismicity of region	D the repairing and protecting of pipelines
5. underground communication	E a pipeline running from a well to a larger line in the field
6. working drawing	F survey that is operated on the pipeline worksite
7. raw materials	G maps of pipeline construction
8. maintenance	H making a map of the field
9. flow line	I factors of earthquake in a certain region
10. gathering line	J a diagram showing the development of a pipeline through different processes in a series

Part Two Listening

Listen to the following passage and fill in the blanks.

Oil and gas pipeline systems are ___1___ for their ___2___ and low transportation cost. A number of studies of ___3___ efficiency have been made. The results vary widely. A recent more thorough investigation ___4___ that crude trunk lines ___5___ about 4.0% of the energy of the crude transported per 1,000 km. Products pipelines use about 0.5% of the energy of the ___6___ moved per 1,000. These rates are ___7___ with estimates of 0.8% for coal trains, 1.0% for oil movement by rail; 2.0% for natural gas pipelines; 3.2% for oil trucks; and 5.4% for coal trucks. Energy ___8___ for water transport is not known ___9___ but is estimated to be 0.8% for oil and 1.1% for coal. The study further indicates that ___10___ oil trunk lines consume about 250BTU/ton-mile.

VOCABULARY ASSISTANT

investigation 调查   crude trunk lines 原油干线
products pipeline 成品油管线   estimate 估计
consume 消耗

Part Three Dialogues

Design Limited Period

When prepare to design the working program, the time for carrying out design work is quite important. Look at the following cues, and try to make a dialogue with your partner.

1. As agreed between the parties, the date of receiving complete data should be the starting date for preparing the technical design.
2. In fact, since the time has been agreed upon, the design work will be prepared within 12 months.
3. The time also includes the period for the approval of design work, and we hope you take it into account.
4. Anyway, we'd like to ask you to consider the possibility of preparing the design work two months earlier.
5. We are well aware of your concern, but it is impossible.
6. We can assure you that there won't be any delay.

★ **Dialogue One**

The following is a discussion on limited period and other preparations between a designer and a proprietor. Read it carefully and answer the following questions.

(D=Designer P=Proprietor)

D: Now let's get down to the question of the time schedule for carrying out the design work.

P: As agreed between us, the date of receiving the complete data will be the starting date for preparing the technical design. However, could you prepare the design work one month earlier?

D: Well, it all depends. The design work is to be prepared within 12 months, including the approval period. We are well aware of your concern, but it's almost impossible...

P: I see. That's really difficult... We'd like your detailed project reports, with technical description and first parcel of drawing. They should be prepared before the *stipulated* date.

D: No problem! We've finalized the *elaboration* of the technical part and economic part in due time.

P: Good! We are also concerned with other preparations. How about the *apparatus*?

D: The equipment, assembly tools and construction materials all correspond to new standards. We are responsible for the quality of equipment and observance of the schedule of *erection work*. By the way, you shouldn't hold us responsible for the damage to equipment, such as *idle time*, unloading, maintenance and *preservation* of equipment.

P: I see. We will be in charge of it. And you should guarantee the safe, proper or *uninterrupted operation* of the equipment. Everything will be done on time.

VOCABULARY ASSISTANT

stipulated 规定的
apparatus 设备
idle time 停机[停歇,故障,中断运转]时间
uninterrupted operation 不间断运转

elaboration 详尽的细节
erection work 安装工作
preservation 保护,维护

Now answer the following questions according to the dialogue.

1. The design limited period is strictly scheduled; if one party wants to change it, how would they express their ideas?
2. What are necessary apparatuses for this project?
3. Why should both parties clarify their separate responsibilities?
4. Can you list other preparations for designing work?

★ **Dialogue Two**
● **General Situation of Petroleum Pipeline**

Two students are talking about the general situation of petroleum pipeline.

Jackson: Look at this picture...the pipeline is the main way to transport crude oil and products.

Jeremy: That's right! Pipelines have their own advantages, i.e. large transporting **capacity**; easy to manage; low energy consumption; short transporting distance; safe operation and low cost...

Jackson: I agree with you. Although pipelines are fit for **unidirectional fluid transportation** and less flexible than truck or **barge**, they still play an essential role in transportation. With developing **onshore** and **offshore** oil fields, the long-distance network is growing. Look at this!

Jeremy: Wow... so many types of pipelines!

Jackson: Generally speaking, pipelines fall into three parts—**gathering**, trunk or **transmission** and **distribution. Flow lines**, the first link in transporting chain from producing well to consumers, are used to gathering oil from individual wells for treatment and storage.

Jeremy: Oh, they look small and short, about two or three inches.

Jackson: Right! And the pressure in the pipe is low. The next link in the pipeline chain is gathering lines. They can transport oil from field processing and storage facilities to a large storage tank or tank farm. The tank farm accumulates oil and pumps into long-distance crude trunk line. Usually these gathering systems typically consist of lines ranging from 4 inches to 8 inches in diameter.

Jeremy: And... they operate at a high pressure?

Jackson: Of course. The network of crude trunk lines **comprises** a wide variety of pipe sizes and capacities. Pumps are needed from the beginning to the end of trunk lines. So we can see pump stations for maintaining pipeline pressure.

Jeremy: Oh, I see. Look at this, some sections are wide, and some are narrow in one pipeline. Why are they different?

Jackson: They are designed to handle expected volumes. If new fields must be tied in by a new branch line, the capacity can be increased by installing more pump stations.

Jeremy: Good! I wonder how the pump station operates, too. Shall we discuss it next time?

Jackson: Ok. Thanks a lot!

UNIT 1 PIPELINE EXPLORATION AND DESIGN

> **VOCABULARY ASSISTANT**
>
> capacity 容量   unidirectional fluid transportation 单向流体运输   barge 驳船
> onshore 陆上的   offshore 海上的   gathering 集油(气)管网
> transmission 输油(气)干线管道   distribution 分配管网   flow line 出油(采气)管道
> comprise 包含

Answer the following questions according to the above dialogues.

1. What are the advantages and disadvantages of pipeline transportation?
2. Can you list any pipelines and their functions?
3. Why does a pipeline have different widths?

★ **Dialogue Three**
● **Pipeline Exploration**

Lin Peng is an undergraduate, practicing in a pipeline survey and design company. He's asking Mr. Steward, an experienced engineer, some questions about pipeline exploration.

Lin Peng: Morning, Mr. Steward. Are you free now?

Mr. Steward: Yes. Can I help you?

Lin Peng: I'm not sure of some operations and rules about pipeline *exploration*. Will you give me some tips?

Mr. Steward: Of course. Go ahead!

Lin Peng: Well, there are a few principles to choose the route. Would you make it clear?

Mr. Steward: Mmm…, choosing the route plays a decisive role in pipeline survey. We should choose as straight as possible, with *slowslopes* and good construction conditions. Second, try to avoid intense earthquake sections and other *mineral areas*, and cover less arable land. Pipelines should keep off the railways, towns, factories and buildings.

Lin Peng: I see… I find the survey shouldn't damage the nearby environment. We should take effective measures to reduce air, water and noise pollution.

Mr. Steward: Exactly. And pipelines should be close to road and *grid*, because it is easy to supply power and materials. It also helps to repair and walk on pipelines.

Lin Peng: I will pay more attention to them. Mr. Steward, would you explain the general process in a survey?

Mr. Steward: Sure! The whole process is survey, *primary design* and *shop drawing reconnais-*

sance. Generally speaking, we should execute it step by step. Sometimes, survey and design are operated in turn.

Lin Peng: Then, what should we do first?

Mr. Steward: Before the survey, we must work out the plan and operation steps. To finish the plan, we have to collect lots of data about natural and economic conditions.

Lin Peng: Let me see... natural conditions are weather, geology and...

Mr. Steward: And *hydrology*, *hydrologic geology*, earthquake and so on. The economic conditions, such as traffic, power supply, large mines, labors and supplies of living necessities, should also be carefully watched and collected.

Lin Peng: Ah... I find the survey is a complex task and full of challenge, but we will be more cautious, patient and proud of working on it. Thank you very much, Mr. Steward.

> **VOCABULARY ASSISTANT**
>
> exploration 勘探   slowslope 缓坡   mineral area 矿区   grid 电网
> primary design 初步设计   shop drawing reconnaissance 施工图勘察
> hydrology 水文   hydrologic geology 水文地质

★ Dialogue Four
● Design of Gas Pipeline

Allen and Ricky are talking about design of gas pipeline.

Allen: Well, to calculate the gas flow in a pipeline, we have to account for so many *formulas*, like pressure effects, temperature, pipe diameter and length, specific gravity and...

Ricky: And pipe *roughness* and gas *deviation*.

Allen: You're right! I'm afraid I have to go over the steps to design gas pipeline!

Ricky: Actually I'm not sure, either. Why don't we turn to our experienced designer?

Allen: Sounds great! Let's go!

Allen and Ricky: Excuse me, Mr. Brown, would you please help us explain how to design gas pipelines?

Mr. Brown: Sure! Emm...An early step in gas pipeline or, say, gas *compressor* design, is analyzing the gas steam to be transported or compressed. As we know, natural gas is a mixture of several components. Do you know its components?

Ricky: Yes, you are right. The largest and significant amount is *methane*; and some natural gas contains *nitrogen*, *carbon dioxide*, *hydrogen sulfide* and water.

Allen: These components have different properties which decide the designing of a gas pipeline.

Mr. Brown: Exactly! Only do we clearly calculate the physical properties of natural gas we can design and construct pipes. For instance, the mixture gravity is needed in gas flow equations. Other properties are required for other design steps, including pressure ratio, temperature and pressure and so on.

Ricky: Really a complex process!

Mr. Brown: With the common use of computer program today, the calculation process is becoming easier. You must be a master of computer!

Allen and Ricky: (Laugh...)

Mr. Brown: There are also pipeline design problems involve many branches, sections of different pipe diameters and weights and other complexities. Compression and pumping must be considered; they should be designed as a system.

Ricky: I think the design of gas pipeline will affect the size and number of compressors or pumps. The design of compressors or pumps stations will affect pipeline operation conditions.

Mr. Brown and Allen: Excellent summary!

> **VOCABULARY ASSISTANT**
>
> formulas 公式,规则　　roughness 粗糙度　　deviation 偏差　　compressor 压缩机
> methane 甲烷　　　　nitrogen 氮　　carbon dioxide 二氧化碳
> hydrogen sulfide 硫化氢

Answer the following questions according to the above dialogues and try to sum up useful expressions.

1. What are the main steps to design gas pipelines?
2. What is the decisive factor of pipeline designing?
3. It is a complex process to design a gas pipeline. Do you believe that you will finish it? How can you achieve it?

There are some useful expressions. Can you list more?

Can I help you? / Is there anything I can do for you? / Anything to help?

Yes, please. / That's very kind of you. / That would be fine.

Please don't worry, thank you just the same. / Thanks, but I think I can manage.

I'm afraid I have to... / I'm not sure... / I've got no idea about...

Would you make it clearer? / Could you tell us more about it?

Part Four Reading

Read the passage and translate some sentences into Chinese.

Products Pipelines

The industry's products pipeline system is a **sophisticated** transportation network. Many **segments** of the system are highly flexible in both capacity and the products that can be transported.

One part of this system moves refined petroleum from refineries to storage and **distribution terminals** in consuming areas. Products shipped include the several grades of gasoline, aviation

gasoline, **diesel**, and home heating oils. In the U.S., much of this movement is from Gulf Coast refining centers to the East and Southeast. But significant volumes of these products are also shipped from the Gulf Coast to the upper Midwest. In other countries products pipelines may move refined products from coastal refineries or tanker unloading terminals to the interior of the country to supply populated areas.

Another group of products pipelines is used to transport liquefied petroleum gases (LPG) and natural gas liquids (NGL) from **processing plants** in oil and gas-producing areas to refineries and **petrochemical plants**. In some cases, a mixed stream of liquid **hydrocarbons** separated from natural gas at field processing plants is moved to a fraction plant where the mixed stream is separated (**fractionated**) into individual products, including ethane, propane, and butanes.

Products pipelines can often carry several different products in the same pipeline. Though there is a short length of the pipeline in which two such "**batched**" products may be mixed, operating methods allow the purity of each product to be maintained. Batching is done either with or without a physical barrier separating the two products. Where no physical barrier is used between different products, the difference in density of the two materials maintains the separation (under pressure

and in turbulent flow) with only a short length interval in which mixing occurs. The position of batch and the extent of mixing can be monitored at points along the line by measuring the density of the fluid in the line. Sphere batching is also used. A sphere can be inserted in the pipeline to form a physical barrier between batches of different products to maintain separation.

Movement of more than one product in a single pipeline obviously calls for even more sophisticated monitoring and control than is required for continuous movement of a single product.

Products pipelines must operate at a higher pressure than crude pipelines because the material being transported is lighter than crude. Products being shipped must remain in a liquid phase rather than become a mixture of gas and liquid. If gas allowed entering the liquid pumps on the pipeline, pump efficiency is lowered and pump damage may result. In general, lighter (lower-density) material requires a higher operating pressure to prevent formation of gas in the pipeline. For instance, one products pipeline that moves ethane from ethane extraction facilities to ethylene manufacturing facilities and underground storage sites has a maximum operating pressure of 1,440 **psi**. To prevent **vaporization**, design criteria for this pipeline call for a minimum pump suction pressure of 650 psi. Ethane is the lightest hydrocarbon transported in products pipeline; the pressure at which vaporization occurs decreases as the density of the material being shipped increases.

OCABULARY ASSISTANT

sophisticated 复杂的   segment 部分(这里指管道)
distribution terminals 分配油库   diesel 柴油   processing plant 处理站
petrochemical plant 石油化工厂   hydrocarbon 烃,碳氢化合物
fractionate 精馏   batched 混油   vaporization 蒸发
psi (pounds per square inch) 磅／英寸 2.1 psi=6.895 kPa(千帕)=0.068 atm(大气压)

Please translate the following sentences into Chinese.

1. Many segments of the system are highly flexible in both capacity and the products that can be transported.

2. In other countries products pipelines may move refined products from coastal refineries or tanker unloading terminals to the interior of the country to supply populated areas.

3. Movement of more than one product in a single pipeline obviously calls for even more sophisticated monitoring and control than is required for continuous movement of a single product.

Unit 2

Pipeline Engineering

管道工程

Look through the following words and phrases concerned with pipeline construction. Do you know all of them?

- cleaning the site
- ditching
- stringing pipes
- road-crossing
- river-crossing
- bending
- testing
- line-up and initial welding
- pipeline welding
- welding inspection
- prime coating and wrapping
- lower-in
- tie-in
- backfilling and cleaning up
- electric engineering

Now answer the following questions.

1. Are all of these activities done in any kind of pipeline engineering? If not, which ones are indispensable?
2. Suppose you are a pipeline worker dealing with dangerous operations, what do you think is the most important in your job?
3. According to your understanding, what qualities should a pipeline worker have?

Unit 2
Pipeline Engineering

VOCABULARY ASSISTANT

stringing pipe 布管 backfilling 回填
ditching 挖沟 welding 焊接
line-up 对口 hydro-testing 试压
lower-in 吊管下沟

AIM
- Execution of Pipeline

Part One Word Power

Match words / phrases in column A to the Chinese equivalents in column B.

A	B
1. lowering-in	A 施工带准备
2. testing	B 对口和焊接
3. pipe bending	C 清理
4. pipe cleaning, coating and wrapping	D 回填管沟
5. backfilling the trench	E 吊管下沟
6. right-of-way preparation	F 试压
7. pipeline handling, transportation and stringing	G 挖沟、穿越
8. ditching, crossing	H 清管、涂防腐层、包扎
9. lining-up and welding	I 弯管
10. site cleaning up	J 管道装卸、运输、布管

Fill in the following blanks with the words in Column A.

1. The _____ operation is performed by ditching machines. It is usual to provide a special gang for the road, rail, cannel and river _____ to allow the pipelaying gang to operate continuously.

2. _____ is carried out by backfilling attachments to tractors. It is essential that soft earth is placed over the pipeline before hard materials are replaced.

3. After the trench has been backfilled, the _____ crew collects all surplus materials such as skids, short ends of pipe, empty fuel and other bits and pieces that invariably finish up on

the right-of-way.

4. The term—_____ refers to the cleared and graded working space which might be prepared along the complete length of the pipeline.
5. The pipe must fit the ditch, changes of direction and elevation both require_____ the pipe.
6. All of them are used to keep the pipes tidy, to prevent corrosion and to protect pipes, they are_____.
7. _____ is the transportation and laying down of the pipe joints along the pipeline trench route.
8. The two methods used in pipeline_____ are "stick" welding and "wire" welding.
9. The pipe can be_____ the trench immediately following the application of the coating and wrapping and forming part of that operation.

Part Two Listening

Listen to the following passage about pipeline-handling and stringing, and then fill in the blanks.

The manufacture, shipping, ____1____ and the pipe stringing along the route is a most important ____2____ operation. It can be said that every ____3____ of pipelining is a matter of logistics, the ____4____ of the project depending on having labour, ____5____ and materials in the right place at the right time and in the right ____6____.

The pipe and other construction materials are usually stacked in suitable stockpipes at

_____7_____ points on the route. Selecting these points is an exercise in most _____8_____ and economic use of transporting means, viz, rail, road, water and air. Pipe stringing is the transportation and laying down of the pipe _____9_____ along the pipe trench _____10_____.

Part Three Dialogues

★ Dialogue One

(*On the Construction Site*)

Tom: Welcome to our worksite! I am in charge of this section. Well, this is a plot plan flow diagram. Would you please give us suggestions on improving it?

Mr. Black: Let me see...How is everything going with this project?

Tom: Everything goes smoothly, and the project has made steady and rapid progress. The laying of the pipelines is being executed fairly well.

Mr. Black: Good! Please introduce the laying procedure briefly.

Tom: Above all, the operations and timing should be planned carefully, and the next day's operation is appointed. Then, the right-of-way crew makes it the road ready for other crews to follow. Next, the stringing and ditching begin. After the crew weld and wrap the pipeline, the backfilling and clean-up crew start their work.

Mr. Black: Quite exact! Then, how many man-days do you need to complete?

Tom: About five thousand man-days.

Mr. Black: Ok. Please pay more attention to safe operation rules whenever and wherever. Meanwhile, we would increase efficiency and shorten the time limit.

Read the above dialogue carefully and answer the following questions, then make up a short dialogue by reference to the language expressions in the box.

1. Before all the operations of construction, what should be arranged carefully?
2. And what experience can you obtain during the arranging process?
3. Sum up the main procedure of laying the pipeline.

Useful Expressions

I'm in charge of this section / project.

Can I help you? / What can I do for you?

What do you expect to know?

How is everything going with this project?

Very well. / Smoothly. / We have some difficulty in ditching.

We need 500 man-days to complete this project.

Thank you for your suggestion.

Thank you, and we will do our utmost to finish it.

According to the above expressions and the following passage, please make a dialogue with your partner to fit the situation of right-of-way preparation.

Right-of-way preparation refers to the *legal acquisition* of the pipeline route, the cleared and *graded* working space, which must be prepared along the complete length of the pipeline. In cultivated areas, advance parties are required to *erect temporary fences* and gates along the line of the right-of-way, and in irrigated country it is necessary to construct temporary bridges over cannels and ditches for the passage of the spread equipment and vehicles. After clearing, the right-of-way must be graded to provide a reasonable road for *wheeled and tracked equipment*. In mountainous countries, the pipeline route may lie along the side of a hill as extensive side hill *excavation* required.

VOCABULARY ASSISTANT

right-of-way preparations 施工带准备
legal acquisition 合法用地   grade 平整
erect temporary fences 设置临时墙
wheeled and tracked equipment 轮式和履带式设备
excavation 开挖

★ Dialogue Two
● Ditching and Trenching

Two young workers, George and Wang Ming, are talking about ditching and trenching.

George: Well...Ming, look at the ground! Rocks are everywhere...

Wang Ming: Yes, it's really difficult for ditching, but don't worry!

          (He picks up a rock and beat it with a hammer.)

George: Ah! It's broken easily!

Wang Ming: Right! They are soft and loosely formed rocks. We may still use our ditching machine, as we did in good ground, and the machine should be preceded by a rooter.

George: I see. The **Rooter** helps to tear up rocks.

Wang Ming: Exactly. However, if the rocks are hard, we have to drill holes along the ditch line and use explosives to break up the rock.

George: Any other facilities?

Wang Ming: **Drill frames** carrying several drills are used. It is handled by **sideboom tractors**. Broken rock is removed by **backhoes**.

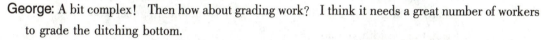
sideboom tractor

George: A bit complex! Then how about grading work? I think it needs a great number of workers to grade the ditching bottom.

Wang Ming: You're right! We are members of them; we should lay in a pad of soft soil so that the pipe can rest on it. The padding can now be done by a special *"padding machine"* which sieves the earth and rejects large stones or rock.

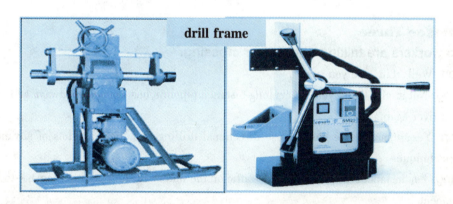
drill frame

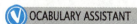OCABULARY ASSISTANT

rooter 犁地机　　drill frame 钻架　　sideboom tractor 履带式吊管机
padding machine 垫土机　　backhoes (有伸缩挖掘装置的)锄耕机

Answer the questions.

1. What technique is necessary where hard rock is encountered?
2. What is the use of "padding machine"?
3. Are "rooters" needed when ditching good ground?

Ditching in rocky countries is complicated. There are other factors in this process. According to the following indications, please make a dialogue with your partner.

a. Ditching should be wide enough to contain the pipe.
b. Ditching must be wide enough to permit the pipeline being lowered in and backfilled without

damage to the pipe or its coating.

c. Ditching should be deep enough to permit the specified cover depth.
d. Ditching must be deep enough to insure it will not interfere with plowing and other normal land use.
e. The excavated soil should be piled up on the left of the opening in order to cover the pipe and backfill.

> ### Useful Expressions
>
> 1. What's your opinion? Are there any good ideas?
> 2. What should we pay attention to when we use the ditching machine?
> 3. I can't agree with you any more!
> 4. Thank you for your advice / kind help! / Thanks anyway!

★ Dialogue Three
● **Two workers are talking about river crossing.**

Johnson: Well, Liu, are you tired?

Liu Gang: Not at all, thank you! Our long-distance pipeline has crossed roadways and streams; now a river again.

Johnson: Yes, this time we have to use directional drilling, for there are lots of advantages of this technique.

Liu Gang: For instance, no disruption of traffic on the waterway, and no little damage to the environment.

Johnson: Right. I remember a crossing under the **Orinoc** River in **Venezuela-distance** of

4550ft. On that project, the drilling rig was positioned so the bit entered the ground at about a 12-degree angle. They drilled a pilot hole and reamed to the desired size. The pipe was pulled through the curved hole.

Liu Gang: A successful crossing! However, we couldn't install pipelines beneath the river every time. Some pipelines are installed on "pipeline bridges"—steel structures to suspend the pipeline above the river.

Johnson: Right! And there must be waterway traffic available. It's really a complex task.

Liu Gang: Do you know the pipeline suspension built across the **Tanana** River in Alaska? It carries the 48 inches trans-Alaska crude pipeline. It spans about 1200ft; the bridge costs about $5 million dollars and was one of 122 river crossings during this pipeline construction.

Johnson: I think if we use the suspension bridge, we also have to consider many factors, such as wind, temperature, freezing of rivers and **seismic shocks** and so on.

Liu Gang: That's true! Whichever method we use, we have to consider these factors. What's more, we must build up confidence!

Johnson: You're right! Nothing is too difficult for us.

> **VOCABULARY ASSISTANT**
>
> Orinoco 奥里诺科河（南美洲北部）
> Venezuela 委内瑞拉
> Tanana 塔那那利佛
> seismic shocks 地震

★ **Dialogue Four**
● **Pipe Cleaning, Coating and Wrapping**

A teacher is talking to his students about methods of pipeline anticorrosion.

Prof. Li: After our discussion about pipe handling, stringing, ditching, trenching and crossings, we should also know some methods of pipeline protection. Do you know ways of pipeline anticorrosion?

Student A: Clean and coat the pipe.

Student B: Wrap the pipe!

Prof. Li: You're right! And we use machines to finish it.

Student A: Would you please tell us the machine and its working process?

Prof. Li: Sure. To clean the pipe, the machine travels along the pipe by its own power. A cradle suspended from sideboom tractor supports

the pipe. The cradle support makes the tractor move along ahead of cleaning machine, thus the cleaning machine can move freely.

Student B: I see. What about other methods?

Prof. Li: The cleaning machine is equipped with a rotating head fitted with cutters and brushes. If there is little dust on pipe surface after cleaning, we should coat primarily. This primer coat can be done by the rear portion of the same cleaning machine.

Student A: Emm... I don't think coating once is enough, Prof. Li.

Prof. Li: It's not enough, another machine also travels along the pipe, using **hot bitumen** or **coaltar** to coat into a fiber glass **reinforcement**. Finally, the pipe is wrapped by **kraft paper**.

Student B: Ah... so it is!

Prof. Li: We have to notice—on short pipelines and on places of **spread working** obstacles, it's necessary to install a stationary coating yard at some point convenient to the pipeline coating. In a word, each pipeline project must consider its own problems, both technical and economical aspects.

Student A and B: Thank you very much, Prof. Li.

VOCABULARY ASSISTANT

hot bitumen 热沥青　　coaltar 煤焦油　　reinforcement 加固材料
kraft paper 牛皮纸　　spread working 综合施工

Part Four　Reading

Pipeline Industry

One of the most important links in the chain of operation that brings oil and gas from the **reservoir** (油藏) to users around the world is a network of pipelines that transports oil, natural gas, and other products from producing fields to consumers. This network, gathering oil and gas from hundreds of thousands of individual wells including those in remote and hostile areas, eventually distributes a range of products to individuals, residences, businesses, and plants.

This vast gathering and distributing system comprises hundreds of thousands of miles of pipelines—almost a half million miles in the U.S. alone—varying in size from 2 inches in diameter to as much as 60 inches. Though pumping stations and other facilities are scattered along pipeline routes, most of the world's oil and gas pipeline system is not visible. Pipelines bring oil from

Alaska and oil and natural gas from **Siberia** to consumers. Oil and gas produced from offshore wells are brought also by pipeline, often through water several hundred feet deep.

Oil and gas pipeline systems are remarkable for their efficiency and low transportation cost. Just as remarkable is the technology that makes it possible to install large pipelines in areas such as the Arctic **permafrost** and deep water regions without damage to the environment and with a high water degree safety.

In addition to bring a low cost transportation method, pipelines are energy efficient. A number of studies of energy efficiency have been made. A recent, more thorough investigation concludes that crude lines consume about 0.4% of the energy content of the crude transported per 1,000 km. Product pipelines use about 0.5% of the energy content of the products moved per 1,000 km. In that rates are compared with estimates of 0.8% for coal trains; 1.0% for oil movement by rail; 2.5% for natural gas pipelines; 3.2% for oil trucks; and 5.4% for coal trucks.

The link between pipeline size and economy is apparent. The relationship between size and capacity is also dramatic. A 36-inch diameter line can carry up to 17 times more oil or gas than a 12 inches diameter pipeline, but construction and operation costs do not increase at nearly the same ratio.

Oil and gas are not the only materials transported by pipeline. Coal and other solids are successfully pipelined today as well.

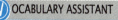

OCABULARY ASSISTANT

    reservoir 油藏   Siberia 西伯利亚   permafrost 永久冻结带

Are these statements true (T) or false (F)? Write T or F in the brackets.

( ) 1. A network of pipeline is one of the most important ways to transport gas and oil from the reservoir to users.

( ) 2. There are no pipelines in the most remote and hostile areas.

( ) 3. The vast gathering and distribution system comprises only several hundreds of miles of pipelines.

( ) 4. The oil pipeline system is remarkable for its low transportation cost.

( ) 5. People install large pipelines in Arctic permafrost region without damage to the environment.

( ) 6. Coal and other solids can't be pipelined today.

Equipment Installation

设备安装

Look at the following equipments used in pipeline construction. Could you add more?

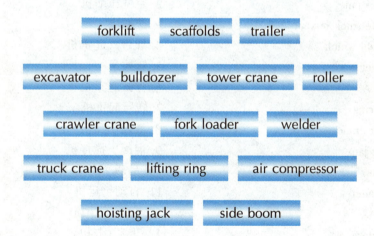

Now answer the following questions.

1. What is the usage of each equipment?
2. Which equipment is the most useful on pipeline construction site?
3. What equipments are often used in pipeline construction site?

UNIT 3 EQUIPMENT INSTALLATION

VOCABULARY ASSISTANT

scaffolds 脚手架　　winch 绞车
crawler 履带牵引装置　crane 起重机
concrete 混凝土　　derrick 动臂起重机
hoist 起重,提升　　jack 千斤顶

AIMS

- Learn different names of equipments and how to operate them

Unit 3
Equipment Installation

Part One   Word Power

Match words / phrases in column A to the Chinese equivalents in column B.

A	B
A. float crane	1. 推土机
B. derrick crane	2. 空气压缩机
C. concrete truck mixer	3. 挖掘机
D. electrical winch	4. 履带式起重机
E. bulldozer	5. 塔式吊
F. roller	6. 浮式起重机
G. lifting ring	7. 转臂起重机
H. crawler crane	8. 液压千斤顶
I. hoisting jack	9. 混凝土搅拌机
J. scaffolds	10. 吊环
K. fork loader	11. 自动铲运机
L. forklift	12. 起重千斤顶
M. excavator	13. 卡环(卡扣)
N. truck crane	14. 电动绞车
O. tower crane	15. 叉式装载机
P. air compressors	16. 吊钩
Q. motor scraper	17. 汽车起重机
R. hydraulic jack	18. 压路机
S. fastening ring	19. 叉式升降机
T. hanger	20. 脚手架

Part Two Listening

Listen to the passage and fill in the missing words.

With the finishing of the hoisting project, the main ____1____ of the National Stadium for the 2008 ____2____ Games have all been completed.

The key steps of the ____3____ of the main stadium, also called "the Bird's Nest," are moving to the installation of its membranes, fit-ups and decorations, installation of electromechanical ____4____ and the outdoor engineering project.

The hoisting project, ____5____ in the stadium's construction, was arranged into two phases. The main structures' ____6____ project started on October 28, 2005 and ended on August 31, 2006. The sub-structures' hoisting was done between September 17 and November 30, 2006.

The Bird's Nest ____7____ two other major steps this year. On August 31 the welding process was completed on its main steel structures and on September 17, its ____8____ structures were successfully removed. The engineering and technical ____9____ as well as the workers ____10____ many difficulties in the construction process.

VOCABULARY ASSISTANT

membranes 隔膜,隔板   fit-ups 临时舞台
electromechanical 电动机械的
sub-structure 下部(底部,基底)结构

Listen again and try to answer the following questions.

(1) Do you know the other name for National Stadium in Beijing?
(2) Which two phases does the hoisting project of the stadium's construction consist of?

Part Three Dialogues

★ **Dialogue One**
● **Lifting Machines**

Setting: *A foreman is talking to a worker on the site about lifting machines.*

A: What lifting machines are there on this site?

B: We have all kinds of machinery on the job site. Tower cranes, truck cranes, **mobile slewing cranes**, crawl cranes and fork loaders.

A: Which is **available** for unloading a **container** from a **wagon**?

B: How many tons does the container weigh?

A: About seven tons.

B: **In that case**, you'd better use the eight-ton capacity mobile crane.

A: But the wagon is at the railway station, it's quite a way from here.

B: Well. You can use truck crane instead. This truck crane can lift a weight of 10 tons. Besides, it travels faster.

A: I will follow your advice.

VOCABULARY ASSISTANT

mobile slewing crane 悬臂汽车吊
available 可利用的   container 货柜
wagon 货车   in that case 既然那样

Read the above dialogue carefully and answer the following questions, then make up a short dialogue with your partner to fit the following situation.

(1) What are the lifting machines on the site?

(2) What kind of lifting machine is recommended at last?

A: 搅拌机运到工地没有？   B: 还没有，没有汽车。

A: 你知道，正急着用呢。   B: 是的，我知道，正在想办法。

A: 搅拌机是什么轮子的？滚子还是轮胎？ B: 轮胎。

A: 我们可以拖，不行吗？   B: 行，但是没有拖拉机。

A: 可以用斗式装载机拖。   B: 好吧，让我们试试看。

★ **Dialogue Two**

● **Hoisting and Mounting**

Settings: An inspector is talking to a worker about the safety of hoisting equipment.

A: Has the **brake device** of the crane been examined?

B: Yes. It has been examined. No problem.

A: Be careful, don't break the equipment. You'd better put it down slowly.

B: O.K. Don't worry about it.

A: May this crane be used to hoist an object of three tons?

B: Of course, the **maximum** lifting weight is 5 tons.

A: Is the **wire rope** safe?

B: There is no problem. There is 5 times safety **coefficient**.

A: Don't stay under the crane boom, please.

B: I'm sorry. Thank you.

VOCABULARY ASSISTANT

brake device 刹车装置
maximum 最大极限的
wire rope 钢丝绳
coefficient 系数

Discuss with your partner with the help of the following specification: What is the general requirement for pipeline equipment installation?

1. The equipment installation includes transportation, lifting, **emplacing**, **grouting** and equipment tightening in place.
2. All the equipments and materials will be transported from the seaport to the temporary storage place or to the construction field directly. At the same time, the material will be inspected to sign the claim damaged report if necessary.
3. The antirust, grease and painting protection things for the equipment will be removed before the equipment installation.
4. Before installation, the flange, pipe end, **wiring box**, **shaft coupling** and other connections with the outer parts will be compared with the drawings.
5. The grouting work will be completed according to the regulation and the technical specifications.
6. The vendor should assign the engineer experienced with the equipment installation to direct in the field during the assembly and start-up of the special equipments.

VOCABULARY ASSISTANT

emplace 安放,安置   grout 用薄泥浆填塞   wiring box 配线盒
shaft coupling 联轴器

Do the following exercises by translating the Chinese into English.

1. A: 这台设备的安装工作何时完成?
   B: It will be completed in three more days. And then it will undergo the stage of systematic pressure testing.
2. A: Who is the director of the installation work?
   B: 王工程师今天负责安装工作。
3. A: 彻底检查一下工具,弄清楚它们是否都处于良好状态。
   B: O.K., we have checked over them all.
4. A: The truck crane can't enter the site because the soil is too spongy.
   B: 我马上平整,然后铺上钢板。
5. A: What is the trouble with the machine?
   B: 我感到这台机器震动严重。

★ **Dialogue Three**
● **Objects Hoisting**

Setting: *A foreman is asking a crane operator to hoist some equipments.*

A: Have you finished **mounting** the truck crane?
B: Yes. It was **assembled**.
A: Can we use it now?
B: Sure, what need to be lifted up?
A: Machine tools, welders.
B: Will those scaffolds be hoisted or not?
A: Yes. And also those pipes.
B: Ok, let's get down to work now.
A: Try to lift them all up before noon!
B: All right, I will do my best.

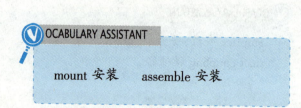

VOCABULARY ASSISTANT

mount 安装   assemble 安装

Use the correct form of the words from the box to complete the sentences.

| machinery | switch | erection | reliable | adjust |
| operate | instruction | compel | out of order | abnormal |

a. We shall put the machine to trial after the _____ work has been finished.
b. We should start the installation according to the _____ and operation manual.
c. The machine is _____, will you see to it, please?
d. Loaders, forklifts and air compressors are heavy construction _____.
e. You must turn off the _____ when anything goes wrong with the motor.
f. These instruments are being _____ by the operator.
g. The lifting work on site will be _____ to stop, owing to the strong wind.
h. Can you _____ this forklift truck?
i. The concrete mixer is steady in quality and _____ in performance.
j. If any _____ temperature arises, it is necessary to stop the machine and investigate the cause.

VOCABULARY ASSISTANT

trial 试车
see to 查看

The following is the valve installation sequence, could you put them in correct order? Then match the sentences (a-g) with each step.

prefabricating
entirety pressure test
checking
anticorrosion
connections
lifting in place
clearance

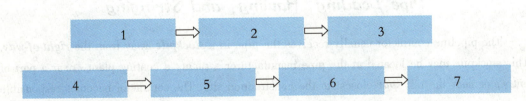

a. _____Prefabricating: The entirety **prefabrication** will be done for valve installation, they will be prefabricated in plant according to the drawings, or on prefabricating flat form set up by steel structure in field.

b. _____Entirety pressure test: The test pressure is consistent with the main pipeline, and the test procedure is according to the station field procedure.

c. _____Checking: Check all valves and their bodies to be surface smooth, clean and no defects existing. The related fittings should be in good condition. Otherwise they aren't allowed to be used. The gears of power driven valve should be clean with no rust or crack existing. The teeth are ensured to be in good condition and the driving and electric parts should be flexible.

d. _____Lifting in place: The safe lifting method for valve and the related fittings in place installation will be used. The lifting work should be stable, care up and down, and put in place according to designed installation position. The valve can be put on the foundation of insulating layer.

e. _____Anticorrosion: The buried pipeline and valves in valves stations should be insulated according to the design requirement, and holiday detection will be done before backfilling.

f. _____Clearance: After the valve room earthwork and process installation in valve stations, the construction **flotsam**, garbage, dirty grease will be cleaned soon and the site will be restored to its original state. The **vertical collocation** will be done according to the design drawings.

g. _____Connections: The connection welding work between valve station and the main pipeline should meet the requirement of welding inspection designation and the related regulations of welding procedure.

> **VOCABULARY ASSISTANT**
>
> prefabrication 配件预制
> flotsam 废料,零碎物
> vertical 垂直的,直立的
> collocation 排列,配置

Part Four Reading

Read the following passages and then answer the questions.

Passage 1

Pipe Loading, Hauling, and Stringing

The pipeline contractor usually receives the pipe in a **stockpile** away from the **right-of-way**. This stockpile may be located at the pipe manufacturer's plant, a coating plant, near a port of entry, or near the rail **spur** closest to the construction site. The contractor becomes responsible for the pipe as it is removed from the stockpile, and remains responsible for all loss and damage until the finished pipeline is accepted by the pipeline company. As each load is removed from the stockpile, a *tally* form is filled out that documents the length, wall thickness, and grade of each joint as well as records any damage. Multiple copies are made for the contractor and the inspection staff. A crane is used to load the pipe on

trucks. The trucks then haul the pipe to the right-of-way where it is off-loaded with a *sideboom* and placed on wooden *skids*, end-to-end, on the right-of-way. The pipes are angled slightly to allow end hooks to be removed and to prevent damage to *bevels*.

Special *precautions* are required to prevent damages to the pipe or coating. These precautions include using rubber or other suitable material between the pipe and the *tie-down* chains, using

padded bunks, and covering the pipe load with *tarpaulins*. Pipes will not be strung until trench *blasting* is completed.

A typical stringing crew would include a foreman, operators, laborers, and truck drivers.

Equipment consists of a crane, a side boom complete with a stringing boom, pipe transport trucks, a *tow* tractor, a 4×4 *pickup*, and crew cab trucks.

The number of trucks needed vary depending on hauling distances and daily production requirements. Pipe may have to be loaded on special pipe carriers for transport in wet areas. Double-jointed pipes (lengths to 25 meters/80 feet) require self-steering *trailers*.

Inspectors monitor the stringing process to ensure that:
- Pipes are being handled so as to prevent damage to it or to the coating, and that the damage is clearly marked.
- Different pipe wall thickness/grades as marked on alignment sheets are correctly placed.
- Public roads and land are not to be damaged by pipe hauling.
- Pipes are not placed on the ground or dragged over it.
- Temporary stockpiles are safe and properly supported.
- Proper end hooks are being used to load and unload pipe to prevent damage to bevels.
- Required gaps are made for access across the right-of-way for the landowner, livestock/wildlife.
- Tallies are accurate and distributed according to procedures.

VOCABULARY ASSISTANT

stockpile 仓库	right-of-way 道路用地,施工带	spur 铁路支线,地方铁路
tally 记账;标签	sideboom 履带式起重机	skids 枕木,垫木
bevel 坡口	precautions 预防,警惕	tie-down 系住,拴住
padded 填补的	bunk 铺位	tarpaulins 防水油布
blasting 爆破	tow 拖	pickup 小型轻便货车
trailer 拖车		

Questions:

1. Where is the stockpile usually located?
2. What equipments are used to load and unload the pipes?
3. What special precautions are required to prevent damage to the pipe or coating?

Passage 2

Handling and Storage of Pipes and Materials

Handling of pipe and other materials shall include all operations by which pipe and materials are handled, such as loading, unloading, hauling, stringing, laying, lowering-in, etc. and all lifting or lowering from one level to another.

Pipe shall always be handled with care and by means of suitable equipment to prevent damages to pipe walls, pipe ends and pipe coating. Pipe shall not be dropped, thrown, dragged, *skidded*, rolled or handled with unsuitable equipment.

a. Pipe handling equipment

Pipe shall always be handled by means of special pipe handling equipment suitable for the specific pipe size being handled. Coated pipes shall be handled with wide *canvas* or *nylon slings*. Bare cables, chains, hooks, *tongs*, metal bars and other unpadded equipment shall not be allowed to come into contact with the coated pipe surfaces. Coated pipe shall only be supported on padded skids or other padded supports, such as plastic covered earth *berms*.

Belts and slings shall have a minimum width equal to the pipe diameter and shall provide

pipe-to-sling *interior angles* of thirty degrees minimum, and shall be of a design that permits rapid and easy removal, such as removable *pin* and *clevis* on one end. Damaged or worn belts or slings shall be *discarded*.

Lifting shoes shall be of *malleable* iron or other approved material and shall be faced with belting material, *brake lining*, plastic or other approved material. They shall be at least 100 mm wide and shall be properly shaped and sized to engage at least one tenth (1/10) of the internal pipe diameter.

End hooks shall have smooth faces and be of a type of material that will not cause damage or contaminate the surface of the pipe. They shall be shaped to properly fit the **curvature** of the inside of the pipe. The cable angle to the vertical shall not exceed 45° without the use of a **spreader bar**.

b. Loading and hauling

Pipe shall only be loaded and hauled on flat bed trucks or special pipe trailers fitted with **bolsters** padded with tough **pliable** material. The bolsters shall be of suitable width and shape to evenly distribute pressure on the pipe. They shall preferably be shaped to support at least thirty degrees of **arc** of the **circumference** of the pipe. Metal bolsters shall not be used. Steel banded truck beds shall be padded, or suitable wooden skids with padding shall be properly placed on such trucks.

The lowest **tiers** of pipe shall be laid on the bolsters and subsequent tiers shall be laid with adequate padding between the pipe layers. Metal to metal contact shall be avoided.

Each length of pipe shall be lowered into position without dropping in order to **nest** evenly with the other lengths. Sudden impact between lengths of pipe or between pipe and other objects shall be avoided.

Each load of pipe shall be tied down using ties of suitable proportions and strength, arranged in such manner that tie-down is achieved over the bolsters. Tie-downs shall be well padded with rubber or similar material, or padded blocks shall be used between the pipe lengths and ties. After the pipe load has been hauled a short distance, any tie-downs that become loose as a result of load settling shall be re-tightened.

To avoid damage to pipes by rocks or other debris thrown up during transit, suitable protective covers shall be placed over the outside of the pipes when they are on a truck or trailer.

c. Unloading

Pipe shall be unloaded from trucks using a side-boom tractor, crane, or forklift with padded bars or **grips**. The pipes remaining on the truck during unloading shall be kept under strict control at all times.

In rocky areas and in unlevelled terrain, pipe shall be unloaded onto suitable pads, padded skids, or plastic covered earth berms to avoid damage from rocks and uneven loading distribution.

d. Storage of pipe

The pipe may stockpile on the right-of-way or at permitted storage locations. The pipe lengths shall be placed on padded timber skids or plastic covered earth berms off the ground at a height that will maintain the pipe above the level where surface or run-off water may contaminate the pipe bevels or flow through the stored pipe. The contact area of pipe and skid and the skid spacing under the pipe shall be sufficient to prevent **denting** or permanent **deformation** of the pipe. Skids shall not be less than 100 mm wide. Pipes on skids shall be **chocked** and blocked to prevent shifting.

The external coating of pipe shall be protected from ultraviolet degradation during storage and during all other stages of construction where pipe is to be left exposed to sunlight for an accumulative period longer than 150 days. Methods of protection shall be in accordance with the coating manufacturer's recommendations.

VOCABULARY ASSISTANT

skid 滑向一侧
sling 钩悬带,吊索
berm 护道,傍山道
pin 钉,栓,销
discard 丢弃,抛弃
malleable 有延展性的,可锻的
brake lining 制动衬面
spreader bar 平压机
pliable 柔软的
circumference 圆周
nest 使套入
dent 凹下,凹进
chock 用楔子垫
canvas 帆布
nylon 尼龙
tong 钳子,夹具
interior angle 内角
clevis U 形夹,马蹄铁
curvature 弯曲;曲率
bolster 垫子
arc 弧,弓形
tier 列,行,排,层
grip 把手,柄
deformation 变形

Questions:

1. What does handling of pipe and materials include?
2. What will be used to unload pipe from trucks?
3. How to unload pipe in rocky areas and in unleveled terrain?

Unit 4

Anticorrosion Pipeline
管道防腐

Look at the following terms involved in pipeline corrosion and anti-corrosion. Could you add more?

- atmospheric corrosion
- electrochemical corrosion
- bitumen coatings
- PVC coatings
- galvanic corrosion
- localized corrosion
- electrolytic corrosion
- polyethylene coatings
- stray current corrosion
- interference corrosion
- concentrated corrosion
- corrosion protection
- epoxy resin coatings
- microbiologically influenced corrosion
- coal-tar enamel coatings

Now answer the following questions.

1. How many types of pipeline corrosions do you know? What are the causes of each of them?
2. Suppose you are applying coatings to pipes in plants, what basic steps will you follow?
3. According to your understanding, what qualities should a coating operator have?
4. Please name some equipments and tools for anticorrosion.

VOCABULARY ASSISTANT

bitumen 沥青   galvanic 电流的,(电池)电流的   electrolytic 电解的
polyethylene 聚乙烯   stray current 杂散电流   epoxy resin 环氧树脂
microbiological 微生物学的   coal-tar enamel 煤焦油搪瓷

AIM

- Grasp various kinds of anticorrosion methods

Unit 4
Anticorrosion Pipeline

Part One Word Power

Match words / phrases in column A to the Chinese equivalents in column B.

A	B
A. microbiologically influenced corrosion	1. 电解腐蚀
B. corrosion protection	2. 电池作用腐蚀
C. concentrated corrosion	3. 微生物腐蚀
D. stray current corrosion	4. 防腐
E. atmospheric corrosion	5. 杂散电流腐蚀
F. uniform corrosion	6. 煤焦油搪瓷涂层
G. bi-metallic / couple corrosion	7. 干扰腐蚀
H. galvanic corrosion	8. 集中腐蚀
I. localized corrosion	9. 大气腐蚀
J. electrolytic corrosion	10. 应力腐蚀
K. stress corrosion	11. 均匀腐蚀
L. interference corrosion	12. 局部腐蚀
M. coal-tar enamel coatings	13. 聚氯乙烯涂层
N. bitumen coatings	14. 环氧树脂涂层
O. polyethylene coatings	15. 阴极保护
P. PVC coatings	16. 沥青涂层
Q. epoxy resin coatings	17. 电化学腐蚀
R. metal coatings	18. 聚乙烯涂层
S. cathodic protection	19. 双金属腐蚀
T. electrochemical corrosion	20. 金属镀层

Part Two Listening

Listen to the passage about internal corrosion of gas transmission pipeline and fill in the missing words.

Corrosion can ___1___ on the internal wall of a steel pipeline when liquid ___2___ within the pipeline. Whether corrosion occurs in these circumstances ___3___ on the nature and amount of contaminants inside the pipeline and the operating ___4___ of the pipeline. Among the actions that an operator must take to prevent corrosion are the use of inhibitors in the gas, the use of cleaning pigs, the ___5___ of liquids and solids from drips, and ___6___ the contaminants. When an operator discovers internal corrosion, an operator must take extra steps such as using coupons to check for corrosion to prevent internal corrosion-induced failure.

Internal corrosion has been one of the three leading causes of the ___7___ incidents in gas transmission pipelines for the past five years, both in ___8___ of incidents and their consequences. To ensure safe and reliable ___9___ of gas, pipeline operators must be vigilant in preventing internal corrosion and monitoring its impact when it occurs. Early planning for corrosion control at the design and construction stage would ___10___ the O&M (operation and maintenance) actions needed later for corrosion control.

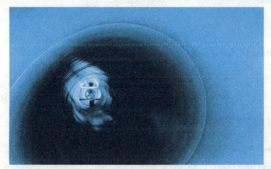

VOCABULARY ASSISTANT

contaminant 污染物
cleaning pig 清管器
inhibitor 抑制剂
coupon 取样管, 试样棒
vigilant 警惕的

Listen again and try to answer the following questions.

(1) Can corrosion occur on the internal wall of a steel pipeline?
(2) When does corrosion occur on the internal wall of a steel pipeline?
(3) What actions should an operator take to prevent corrosion?

Part Three Dialogues

★ Dialogue One
● Coating application on pipes

A: Today, we are going to apply external coatings on pipes.
B: What shall we do first?
A: Well, the first thing to do is to fix the pipes on a **bracket** and clean the surface of the pipes.
B: All right, the dust can be removed from the surface **utilizing compressed air**. How about the **grease**?
A: Use **detergent** to **eliminate** any grease on the surface of materials.

B: What is next?

A: The primer shall be applied from two ends by means of **spraying** at the same time. Use the same method to spray the surface layer of paint. And the coated steel surface shall be protected by paper tapes or packing tapes.

B: After coating is finished, it needs to be **solidified**, isn't it?

A: Quite right. Besides, the coating shall be protected from contaminant during solidification.

B: After it is dry completely, can the pipe be transported to the site for construction?

A: Sure.

VOCABULARY ASSISTANT

bracket 托架,支架　utilize 利用
compressed air 压缩空气
grease 油脂　detergent 清洁剂
eliminate 除去　spray 喷射
solidify (使)凝固

(1) Before applying the coating material, what should be done?

(3) Sum up the main procedure of the pipe coating.

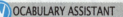

A: 这里用什么做涂层?
B: 是用煤焦油。
A: 这里有空气隔绝层吗?
B: 有,有 20 厘米的空隙。
A: 这里使用泡沫塑料吗?
B: 是的,采用的是聚苯乙烯泡沫塑料。
A: 保温隔热层是多厚?
B: 20 厘米厚。
A: 在使用隔气、保温隔热材料时,应先检查一下。
B: 是,已经检查过了,全部合格。
A: 保温隔热、隔绝材料不要受潮。
B: 放在仓库里了,不会受潮。

VOCABULARY ASSISTANT

air-isolating layer 空气隔绝层
foam plastics 泡沫塑料
polystyrene foam plastic 聚苯乙烯泡沫塑料
thermal insulating layer 保温隔热层

★ **Dialogue Two**

● **Field coating of welded joints.**

A: What coating materials can be used for welded joints?

B: The **heat shrinkable sleeve** (**tape**) is used for the joint coating of the buried pipeline coated with three-layer PE coating.

A: Is there any requirement for the heat shrinkable sleeve (tape)?

B: Yes, the surface of the heat shrinkable tape shall be smooth with no *air bubble*, *pitting*, *crack*, *oxidation-deteriorating* phenomena.

A: Is coating procedure for welded joints the same as pipe coating?

B: Not exactly. When pipe joint is with water stream (or dew), it is necessary to heat the joints with a flame heater to remove water content on pipeline surface.

A: Do we need to clean the welded joint?

B: Of course. After heating, *sandblasting* method shall be used for cleaning the pipe joint. Then, surface dust and foreign matters at the location of joint coating shall be cleaned with soft brush or clean cotton cloth.

A: Is it time to use the heat shrinkable sleeve (tape)?

B: Just one more thing. Heat pipe joint by burning flame *spray gun*. When the temperature reach to the specified point, the matched primer could be sprayed and the heat shrinkable sleeve shall be *wrapped* up on the welded joint rapidly to fix its location.

A: Is that all?

B: Almost. After the heat shrinkable sleeve is located, it will be heated by means of flame heater, when adhesive glue overflows from *axial seam* and *loop seam*, it may be thought to complete installation of the heat shrinkable sleeve.

A: It's so complicated.

B: You will be familiar with that after applying coating for several times.

VOCABULARY ASSISTANT

welded joint 焊接接头
heat shrinkable sleeve (tape) 热收缩带
air bubble 气泡   pitting 蚀损斑
crack 裂缝   oxidation-deteriorating 氧化恶化的
sandblast 喷砂   spray gun 喷漆枪
wrap 缠绕   axial seam 轴向接缝
loop seam 环向接缝

Discuss with your partner with the help of the following procedure: How to proceed site joint coating of pipeline loop welds? What methods can be used to decide whether the coating is eligible?

Procedure: pipe end cleaning → pipe end preheating → sandblasting → pipe end heating → temperature measurement → brushing primer → installing hot shrinkable sleeve (tape) → heating hot shrinkable sleeve (tape) → inspection acceptance → joint coating mark → filling in construction and inspection records

Do the following exercises by translating the Chinese into English.

1. A: 煤焦油在防腐方面起什么作用?
   B: Coal-tar has been playing an important part in preventing pipe from corrosion.
2. A: What method do you take to prevent metal parts from corrosion?
   B: 涂漆可以防止金属零件腐蚀。
3. A: Where should we put these anti-corrosion materials?
   B: 防腐材料应该存储在干燥的地方,避免潮湿和阳光直射。
4. A: What should we do if the pipe fittings become rusty?
   B: 如果管件生锈必须清除掉!
5. A: Why was rust formed on these pipes?
   B: 生锈来自氧对金属的作用。

★ **Dialogue Three**
● **Safety of anticorrosion materials**

Setting: *The follow dialogue is between an inspector and a foreman in the store house before applying the anticorrosion materials.*

A: Are all the anticorrosion materials in accordance with standards?
B: Yes, they were purchased according to standards.
A: The **cementing material** of anticorrosion is **noxious**. We should pay attention to safety.
B: The **articles** for protection have been provided.
A: Some of the anticorrosion materials are **inflammable**. You should take good care of them.
B: Yes, I see.
A: During construction of **ethylene perchloride** is going on, you should be careful with smoke and fire.
B: I've told everybody not to smoke.
A: Near the store-house of cementing material of the anti-corrosion, smoking or lighting fire is strictly forbidden.
B: Yes, there have been the signs of "Fire Forbidden" already.
A: Let's check up the anticorrosion materials first.
B: I've checked them up already. If you like, we can do it again for the sake of safety.

 OCABULARY ASSISTANT

cementing material 胶结料
noxious 有毒的
article 用品
inflammable 易燃的
ethylene perchloride 过氯乙烯

Use the correct form of the words from the box to complete the sentences.

| exterior | damp | rust | corrode | foreign |
| protect | covering | according to | coat | clean |

a. Before any coating is applied, the pipe must be _____.
b. This process removes all mill scale, rust, dirt and other _____ matter.
c. All dust is cleaned from the primed pipe before it is _____.
d. The machine sprays a protective coating of coal tar or asphalt base over the entire _____ wall of the pipe.
e. Repairs requiring uncovering and _____ a second time are expensive.
f. Anticorrosion materials shall be stored in dry places and prevented from _____ and exposing in sunlight.
g. If you take good measures to prevent corrosion, _____ will not be formed on the pipeline fittings.
h. Pipes are often _____ by the oxygen in the air.
i. Well _____ from corrosion, these pipes are not rusty at all.
j. The anticorrosion construction of buried pipeline and valves and fittings shall be carried out _____ the design documents.

VOCABULARY ASSISTANT

primed 涂底漆的
uncovering 开挖
fitting 配件

The following is the anticorrosion sequence in plants, could you put them in correct order? Then match the sentences (a-i) with each step.

cleaning surface   spraying paint
preparation   blast cleaning
checking and acceptance
solidifying
filling in construction records
portage and placement
removing dust

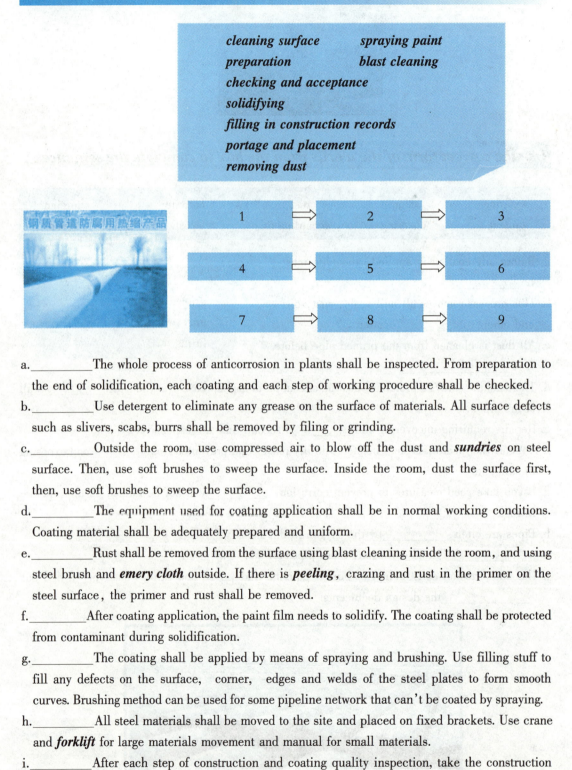

1 ⇒ 2 ⇒ 3
4 ⇒ 5 ⇒ 6
7 ⇒ 8 ⇒ 9

a._____ The whole process of anticorrosion in plants shall be inspected. From preparation to the end of solidification, each coating and each step of working procedure shall be checked.

b._____ Use detergent to eliminate any grease on the surface of materials. All surface defects such as slivers, scabs, burrs shall be removed by filing or grinding.

c._____ Outside the room, use compressed air to blow off the dust and **sundries** on steel surface. Then, use soft brushes to sweep the surface. Inside the room, dust the surface first, then, use soft brushes to sweep the surface.

d._____ The equipment used for coating application shall be in normal working conditions. Coating material shall be adequately prepared and uniform.

e._____ Rust shall be removed from the surface using blast cleaning inside the room, and using steel brush and **emery cloth** outside. If there is **peeling**, crazing and rust in the primer on the steel surface, the primer and rust shall be removed.

f._____ After coating application, the paint film needs to solidify. The coating shall be protected from contaminant during solidification.

g._____ The coating shall be applied by means of spraying and brushing. Use filling stuff to fill any defects on the surface, corner, edges and welds of the steel plates to form smooth curves. Brushing method can be used for some pipeline network that can't be coated by spraying.

h._____ All steel materials shall be moved to the site and placed on fixed brackets. Use crane and **forklift** for large materials movement and manual for small materials.

i._____ After each step of construction and coating quality inspection, take the construction records seriously.

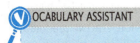

OCABULARY ASSISTANT

sundries 杂物   emery cloth 金刚砂布
peel 剥皮   forklift 铲车

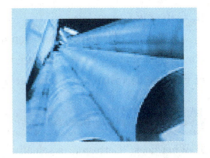

Part Four   Reading

Read the following passages and then answer the questions.

Passage 1

Causes of Underground Corrosion

In any discussion of corrosion of underground iron or steel structures, a number of basic truths must be understood and accepted.

Corrosion of iron and steel is a natural process. Underground corrosion of iron and pipes is often viewed as an unusual condition that occurs as a result of unusual circumstances and environments. Actually, corrosion occurs whenever iron or steel is placed underground. Because iron is not stable in its refined state, it can be expected to become iron oxide (rust) eventually. The energy that is *imparted* to the metal during the refining process seeks to be released, thus allowing the metal to revert to the ore from which it was derived.

It was reported that all *ferrous metals* corrode essentially at the same rate. The apparent corrosion resistance of *cast iron pipe is attributed to* the fact that *graphitized* cast iron can retain its appearance as a pipe even though much of the iron is gone.

Corrosion is selective and concentrated. The basic corrosion occurs only at anodic areas and does not distribute over the entire metal surface. These anodic areas are relatively small compared to the cathodic or uncorroded areas. Even in severely corroded pipelines with numerous leaks, less than 5% of the total surface area is attacked.

Once leaks start to occur, they continue to occur at a sharply rising rate.

Two basic forms of electrochemical corrosion mechanisms are responsible for underground corrosion: electrolytic and galvanic.

A. Electrolytic Corrosion

Electrolytic corrosion is a result of direct current from outside sources. These direct currents are introduced into the soil and are picked up by an underground pipe. The locations where the current is picked up are not affected, or at least are provided some degree of corrosion protection.

B. Galvanic Corrosion

Although electrolytic corrosion can result in very rapid deterioration and must be dealt with almost immediately, it is encountered far less frequently than galvanic corrosion. The two predominant of galvanic corrosion are dissimilar metals and dissimilar environment.

Now answer the questions.

1. What does "Corrosion is selective and concentrated" mean?
2. What is the basic corrosion mechanism of iron underground?
3. What are the basic forms of iron underground corrosion?

VOCABULARY ASSISTANT

imparted 给予的,授予的
ferrous metal 黑色金属
cast iron pipe 生铁管
be attributed to 归因于
graphitized 石墨化的

Passage 2

Coating

It is a normal practice to apply coating consisting of organic materials to pipelines for corrosion protection purposes. The mechanical protection and the electrical isolation provided by the coating should be as complete as possible. The pipeline will then only be in contact with the soil at points where the coating is damaged during installation or excavations at a later date. To protect the pipeline at such points where the coating is damaged, catholic protection is required. Sand padding provides a good mechanical protection for the pipeline but is not adequate for corrosion protection.

A few years ago, discussions of coatings centered on the question of whether to use bituminous or tar coatings or whether plastic coatings were sufficiently reliable. This is no longer the case: plastic is now the main type of coating material used in all the highly industrialized countries. When selecting a coating nowadays, the question to be answered is which type of plastic coating provides the best solution from a technical and an economic point of view. Other problems which must be resolved are the tests which need to be made in order to determine whether the coating will be sufficiently *resilient* over the long run.

1. Coal-Tar Enamel Coatings

Coal-Tar enamel has certain advantages over bitumen, particularly as regards mechanical stability. However, coal-tar enamel is not used in many countries, mainly because of its unpleasant smell. Also, this type of coating material could not be used for water pipelines, because of the effect on the taste of the water.

2. Bitumen Coatings

Bitumen is now mainly used as a material for relatively thick coating with a glass fibre wrap.

The minimum coating thickness is approx. 4 mm.

A major disadvantage of bitumen coating is its lack of mechanical strength. During pipe shipment, severe coating damage can occur, requiring repairs on site. Because of the lack of mechanical resistance, bitumen-coated pipes must also be installed in soil which is completely free of stones. Because of these disadvantages, plastic coating has now, to a large extent, replaced bitumen.

3. Plastic Coating

(1) Polyethylene Coatings

The plastic coating material mainly used is polyethylene. The major advantages of polyethylene are as follows:

- High mechanical strength
- High electrical resistance
- High resistance to chemicals and aging low *permeability* to oxygen and water wide temperature range.

Polyethylene coatings are mainly applied in two methods:

a) *extrusion* using *annular extruders* or wrapping machines

b) *thermal fusion*

(2) *PVC* Coatings

PVC is not used as a coating material because of its poor low temperature impact properties and other undesirable features such as *saponification* and *plastifier* migration.

(3) Epoxy Resin and *Polyurethane-Tar* Coatings

Epoxy Resin powder is applied to the pipe by an electric process to form a coating with a thickness of only aprox. 300 um.

Polyurethane-Tar is sprayed onto the pipe surface, forming a layer with a thickness of approx. 1.5 mm i.e. thinner than polyethylene but thicker than epoxy resin.

(4) Three-Layer PE Coating

The latest development is a three-layer PE coating consisting of one layer of epoxy resin, a layer of hard adhesive and an outer layer of polyethylene or *polypropylene*.

Answer the following questions.

1. How many types of coatings are mentioned in the article? What are they?
2. What are the advantages of Polyethylene Coatings and disadvantages of Coal-Tar Enamel Coatings?

VOCABULARY ASSISTANT

resilient 有回弹力的　　permeability 渗透性　　extrusion 挤出
annular 环形的　　　　extruder 挤压机　　　thermal fusion 熔化,熔解
PVC 聚氯乙烯　　　　saponification 皂化　　plastify 热塑化
Polyurethane-Tar 聚亚安酯焦油　　polypropylene 聚丙烯

Unit 5

Oil and Gas Transportation

油气集输

Look through the following words and phrases concerned with gas and oil transportation. Learn them by heart and try to add more.

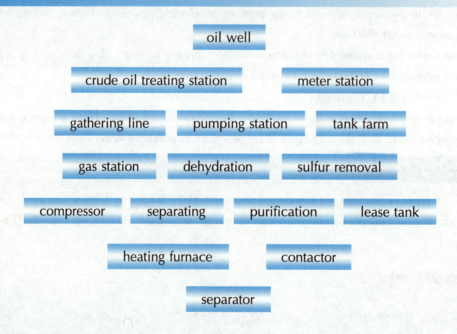

Now discuss the following questions with your partner. Please notice that some of the questions are open-ended.

1. Can you sum up the above terms to different categories? Which ones are stations and which ones

belong to the processing flow?
2. Can you pick out some equipments or facilities from these terms? What are they?
3. How much do you know about oil and gas transportation? Do you know the whole process of it?

VOCABULARY ASSISTANT

crude oil 原油
dehydration 脱水
sulfur 硫
purification 净化
compressor 压缩机

Unit 5
Oil and Gas Transportation

AIMS

- Flow of oil and gas transportation and terms concerned with it

Part One   Word Power

Look at the flow chart of oil and gas transportation. Can you speak out the name of each part in English?

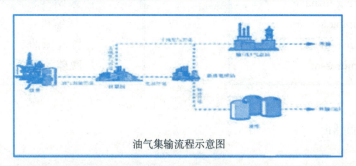

油气集输流程示意图

Match words / phrases in column A to the Chinese equivalents in column B.

A	B
A. oil well	1. 油气混输管道
B. oil and gas transportation pipeline	2. 油库
C. meter station	3. 油井
D. oil gathering line	4. 集油管道
E. crude oil treating station	5. 集气管道
F. oil transmission pipeline	6. 输油管道
G. tank farm	7. 计量站
H. gas gathering line	8. 原油处理站
I. gas station	9. 输气站

Now, can you fill in the flow chart of oil and gas transportation with the above words?

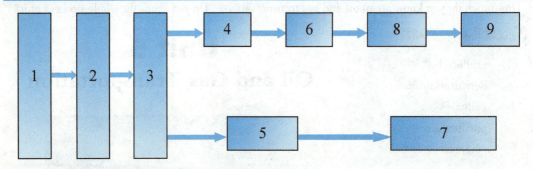

Do you know the following terms related to oil and gas transportation? Match them with their Chinese equivalents and learn them by heart.

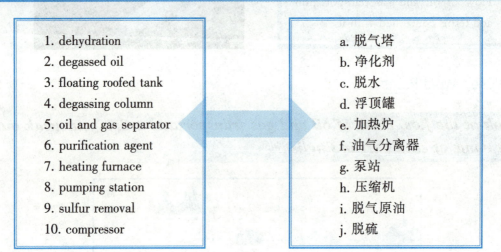

1. dehydration
2. degassed oil
3. floating roofed tank
4. degassing column
5. oil and gas separator
6. purification agent
7. heating furnace
8. pumping station
9. sulfur removal
10. compressor

a. 脱气塔
b. 净化剂
c. 脱水
d. 浮顶罐
e. 加热炉
f. 油气分离器
g. 泵站
h. 压缩机
i. 脱气原油
j. 脱硫

Part Two Listening

Listen to the passages and fill in the blanks with the proper missing words.

Passage 1

When _____1_____ oil is produced, various amounts of _____2_____, water, and other _____3_____ are mixed with the oil. Some of the _____4_____ comes as free oil, some as free water, and some as a _____5_____ mixture known as an _____6_____. The gas, water, and other impurities (known as basic _____7_____ and water) must be _____8_____ before selling the oil. This _____9_____ process is called oil _____10_____.

Listen again and answer the following questions.

1. What are the probable components of crude oil?
2. What is oil treating?

Passage 2

When water and gas have been removed from the oil, it is in lease tanks for ___1___. Oil may be trucked from the ___2___ if a pipeline is not available, but this method is used primarily when small ___3___ of oil are produced on the lease and a ___4___ is not justified, or when a new well is not completed.

Oil leaving the lease must be ___5___, either ___6___ or automatically. Manual measurement involves gauging the lease tanks before and after oil is removed. The volume shipped is then ___7___. Oil can be shipped from the lease by manually operating a valve in the ___8___ tank that lets oil flow into a truck or into the pipeline company's ___9___ line.

Today, lease automatic custody transfer (LACT) units are used where significant oil ___10___ are involved.

Listen again and answer the following questions.

1. How many ways of transporting the oil leaving the lease?
2. When should the oil be trucked instead of being transported in a pipeline?

VOCABULARY ASSISTANT

manually 用手操作地
lease automatic custody transfer 井区自动转输站

Passage 3

The function of ___1___ pipelines and gas ___2___ lines is similar to that of crude-gathering and ___3___ trunk lines respectively, but operating containers and ___4___ are quite different. In general, gas pipelines operate at high ___5___ than crude lines; gas is moved through a gas pipeline by ___6___ rather than by ___7___; and the path of natural gas to the user is more ___8___.

Listen again and answer the following questions.

1. What's the function of the gas pipelines?
   Is there any difference between oil and gas pipelines?

Part Three Dialogues

Read and act out the dialogues with your partner.

Bob (B) is an experienced engineer in the area of oil and gas transportation. He is talking to Wang Lin (W), a beginner of this area.

★ **Dialogue One**

W: Hello! Bob! You know I'm new in this field, so would you please tell me something about it?

B: With pleasure! But what would you like to know first?

W: Well, how many kinds of pipelines are there being used at present?

B: According to their functions, most oil and gas pipelines fall into one of the three groups: gathering, trunk/transmission, and distribution pipelines.

W: So the first type is for collecting crude oil or natural gas?

B: Yes. In the first group, for example, we have flow lines which connect individual oil or gas wells to central treating, storage, or processing facilities within the field.

W: What's the standard size of such pipelines?

B: These lines are usually small-diameter. The size requirements vary according to the capacity of the well being served, the length of the line, and the pressure available at the producing well. And typical ***diameters*** are 5.08 cm, 7.62 cm, and 10.16 cm (2 in, 3 in, and 4 in).

W: I see.

★ **Dialogue Two**

W: How about the trunk/transmission pipelines?

B: This group, just as its name implies, is responsible for the transportation of oil and natural gas. Crude trunk lines, for example, are usually large-diameter and long-distance, and they take the oil from large central storage facilities to other storage ***terminals***.

W: They are also of different sizes?

B: Yes. The network of crude trunk lines comprises a wide variety of pipe sizes and capacities to meet different needs.

W: Different needs?

B: Yeah. Such as different ***volumes***. That is, the different sections of the system are sized to handle expected volumes. And crude trunk lines can be several hundred miles long, and individual sections are joint by welding.

W: That easy? Anything else to do in addition to joining them by welding?

B: Of course it's far more than just joining them together. Pumps, for example, are required at the beginning of the trunk line, and pumping station must be spaced along the pipeline to maintain the required pressure.

W: So, what if new fields must be tied in by a new branch line?

B: In that case, the capacity can often be increased by installing additional pumping station.

W: Then, I guess that control of such a system must be a complex operation.

B: It is indeed. Actually, sophisticated *monitoring* and control systems have been developed to permit the pipeline operator to fulfill delivery *commitments* and avoid a *malfunction* of the system.

W: I think we do need those systems.

B: Certainly.

★ Dialogue Three

W: And how about the gas?

B: The trunk lines of gas?

W: Yeah, I wonder if the gas transmission system is similar to that of oil?

B: Hum...like crude trunk lines, gas transmission systems can also cover large *geographical* areas.

W: You mean it can also be several hundred miles long?

B: Maybe even longer. And they take dry, clean, natural gas from field-processing facilities to cities where it is distributed to individual businesses, factories, and residences.

W: So that will be done with distribution lines?

B: Exactly!

W: And I guess that the distribution lines to the individual users are quite small.

B: Yeah, you're right!

W: And they are *metered*!

B: Of course!

VOCABULARY ASSISTANT

diameter 直径
volume 体积,量
commitment 责任;承担义务
geographical 地理学的,地理的
meter 用表测量[计量,记录];计量[定量]供给

terminal 终点站,终端
monitoring 监视,控制,监测,追踪
malfunction 故障

Act out the dialogues in pairs and then discuss the following questions.

1. How many kinds of pipelines do you know?
2. What does a gathering line do?
3. Do you know the normal size of a gathering line?
4. What are the trunk lines for?
5. Do you know how to control a transmission system?
6. What's a distribution line?

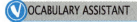
OCABULARY ASSISTANT

homogeneous 同类的,均匀的
emulsion 乳状液
oil emulsion 油品乳化液,油乳胶

Part Four Reading

Passage 1

Storage and Transportation of Oil and Gas

Technical advances have been most spectacular in the transportation of petroleum and petroleum products nowadays. In fact, many oil fields have been discovered in places that are far from the point at which the oil will be refined and used. One has only to think of oil deposits on the shores of the Arctic Ocean or in the jungles on the interior slope of the Amazon Basin to realize  the difficulties that are involved in getting the oil from the well to the consumers. So, that is why steel pipes were developed rapidly.

There are several kinds of pipelines. Flow lines run from the well to a larger line in the field which is called a gathering line. The oil is then carried into a trunk line. The trunk lines transport oil to refineries or to storage areas, usually at ports so that the oil can be shipped by water. The diameters of pipelines vary from about an inch for a flow line to as much as forty-eight inches for one of the major trunk lines.

Some pipelines run above the surface, especially in rugged or uninhabited areas, but many others run beneath the ground. In farming countries with open fields, there may be no surface indication at all the black stream of oil under the growing crops. However, the pipelines are marked by pumping stations at an average distance of about seventy-five miles closer in mountainous areas, farther apart in flat countryside. Special equipment may also be necessary for some pipelines; in the northern part of China, for instance, special heating devices are required to keep the oil from freezing in the intense cold.

Pipelines are cleaned by a device called a pig. This mechanism has metal blades that scrape the inside of the pipe to keep it clean of the *tar-like substance* that forms in it. The pressure of the oil itself forces the pig to move through the pipe. The pig can only go from one pumping station to the next, where it is taken out and cleaned.

The pipelines must be constantly checked. Each section is patrolled by a pipeline walker who looks for evidence of a leak or other damage in the line. It is possible to smell escaping gas or to detect spots where **seepage** has occurred. Nowadays, many "walkers" do their inspecting from low-flying airplanes, since traces of seepage can be seen from the air.

Another type of pipeline has been developed to carry finished products from the refineries to distribution centers. It is called the product pipeline. Strange as it may seem, products as different as gasoline, **benzene**, or kerosene can be carried in the same pipeline with only a very small amount of mixing.

The transportation of oil has also led to the spectacular development of giant ships, the largest ships that have ever sailed the oceans of the world. The supertankers that sail the seas today have so many different compartments that they can carry crude oil and finished products at the same time, or even crude oil from several sources, which may be different chemical mixtures. On many of these huge ships, computers keep track of and perhaps supervise both the loading operation and the navigation.

Other special types of carriers have also been developed for the transportation of oil or oil products. On water, special barges are used for transporting oil on sheltered or inland waterways like lakes, rivers or canals. On land, we have tank cars to transport petroleum by rail. Today, one of the familiar sights on our highways is the tank truck, which is a special kind of vehicle used to carry petroleum or its products.

Passage 2

Petroleum Surface Treatment

Well fluids are often a complex mixture of liquid hydrocarbons, gas, and some impurities, so it's necessary to remove the gas and the impurities from the liquid hydrocarbons before they are stored and transported. Liquid hydrocarbons and objectionable impurities must also be removed from natural gas before the gas goes to a sales line. Impurities that might be found in some well streams are hydrogen sulfide, carbon dioxide, free water, **water vapor**, **mercaptans**, nitrogen, **helium**, and solids. Nearly all of the impurities cause various types of operating problems.

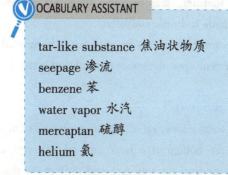

VOCABULARY ASSISTANT

tar-like substance 焦油状物质
seepage 渗流
benzene 苯
water vapor 水汽
mercaptan 硫醇
helium 氦

Oil Treating

The separation of natural gas, liquid hydrocarbons, and impurities is accomplished by various field processing methods, depending upon the composition of the well stream and the desired end product. These methods include time, chemicals, gravity, heat, mechanical or electrical process, and combinations of these. And this separation process is called oil treating.

Treating systems are important parts of lease equipment. In selecting the system, a number of factors should be considered to determine the most desirable method of treating the crude oil to pipeline requirements. Some of the factors are:

> **VOCABULARY ASSISTANT**
> heater-treater 加热处理器
> gun barrel 沉淀罐,油水分离器
> scaling 水垢形成
> paraffin 石蜡
> reverse emulsion 水包油型乳液
> emulsifier 乳化剂
> coalescence 合并

1) Tightness of emulsion.
2) Specific gravity of the oil and produced water.
3) Corrosiveness of the oil, gas and produced water.
4) *Scaling* tendencies of the produced water.
5) Quantity of fluid to be treated and percent of water in the fluid.
6) Availability of sales line for the gas.
7) Desirable operating pressure for the equipment.
8) *Paraffin*-forming tendencies of the equipment.

Oil-field emulsions are usually of the water-in-oil type; however, a few of the emulsions are oil-in-water type and are called *reverse emulsions*. Emulsions are complex and each should be considered individually.

In order to break a crude oil emulsion and obtain clean oil, it is necessary to displace the *emulsifier* and its film. This brings about the *coalescence* of droplets of water and furnishes a means and time of undisturbed settling of the coalesced water drops. There are several methods used in conjunction with one another to treat an oil emulsion.

Heater-Treaters

A *heater-treater* is normally used in treating oil emulsions. It uses thermal, gravity, and sometimes chemical and/or electrical methods to break emulsions.

Heater-treaters can be vertical or horizontal in design. The size is dependent upon the volume of oil and water to be handled.

gun barrel

In some cases, an oil-water emulsion is not very stable and, time permitting, water will settle toward the bottom of a tank and oil will rise to the top. Heat and chemicals may be used to shorten the time for settling, and to improve the separation of the two liquids. The settling vessel is known as a *gun barrel* or wash tank.

The gun barrel comes in various designs; however, it usually has sufficient height to allow the clean oil to gravity-flow into the stock tanks. The water is drawn off through **water leg**, which also regulates the oil-water interface level.

● Storage Tanks

Oil that is free of impurities after certain type of treating and meets the pipeline specifications is called clean oil or pipeline oil. It goes from the treating facilities, such as a separator, a heater-treater, or a gun barrel, to the storage tanks.

The number and size of **storage tanks** depend upon the volume of oil produced each day,

the way that the oil will be sold, and how frequently and at what rate the oil is taken by the pipeline company.

The most commonly used types of tanks at present are **vaulted tanks** and floating roofed tanks (single plate or double plates). And they are of various medium with 10,000–150,000 m³ volume.

● Separators

Separation of well-stream gas from free liquids is the most common and simplest form of field processing. Separator is the equipment most widely used for this type of processing. The separation of natural gas from liquids and/or impurities in a separator combines gravity, time, mechanical processes, and occasionally chemicals.

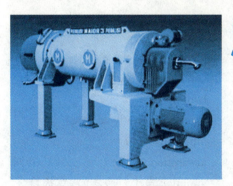

VOCABULARY ASSISTANT

water leg 水夹套,水涨落速度装置
vaulted tank 拱顶罐
storage tank 储油罐
separator 分离器
horizontal 水平的
spherical 球形的

The size of the separator used is dependent upon rate of flow of the natural gas and/or liquids going in the vessel, and separators are built in various designs, such as vertical, *horizontal* and *spherical*. The internals of the vessel, to aid in the mechanical separation of the gas and liquids, are of a special design, depending upon the manufacture. Although most separators are two-phase in design separating the gas and liquids, they can be built three-phase to separate natural gas, liquid hydrocarbons, and free water.

Under certain conditions it is desirable to use more than one stage of separation to obtain more recovery of fluids.

● Dehydration of Natural Gas

Most natural gas contains substantial amount of water vapor at the time it is produced from a well. Even the natural gas separated from an associated crude oil stream may be **saturated** with water vapors. Water vapor must be removed from the gas stream because it will **condense** into liquid and may cause **hydrate** formation as the gas is cooled from the high reservoir temperature to the cooler surface temperature. Liquid water almost always accelerates corrosion, and the solid hydrates may pack solidly in gas-gathering systems, resulting in partial or complete blocking of flow lines.

The term dehydration means removal of water. Water vapor may be removed from natural gas by bubbling the gas **counter-currently** through certain liquids that have a special attraction or **affinity** for water. When water vapors are moved by this process, the operation is called **absorption**. There are also solids that have an affinity for water. When gas flows through a bed of such **granular** solids, the water is **retained** on the surface of the **particles** of the solid material. This process is called **adsorption**. The vessel in which either absorption or adsorption takes place is called the **contactor** or **sorber**. The liquid or the solid having affinity for water and used in the contactor in connection with either of the processes is called **desiccant**.

So, there are two major types of dehydration equipment in use at this time, namely the liquid-desiccant **dehydrator** and the solid-desiccant dehydrator. Each has its special advantages and disadvantages and its own field of particular usefulness. Practically all the gas moved through transmission lines is dehydrated by one or the other of these two methods.

VOCABULARY ASSISTANT

saturate 浸透;使饱和
condense 浓缩,凝结
hydrate 水合物
counter-currently 逆流地
affinity 吸引力
absorption 吸收
granular 由小粒而成的,粒状的
retain 保持,保留
particle 粒子,微粒
adsorption 吸附
contactor/sorber 混合器,萃取器
desiccant 干燥剂
dehydrator 脱水器

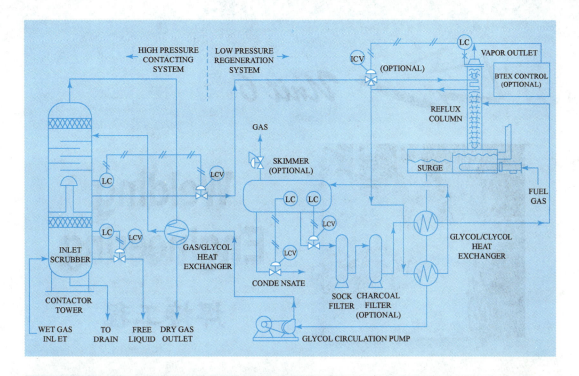

Discuss the following questions after reading.

1. What are the probable elements of well fluids?
2. Why should we remove the impurities from crude oil and natural gas before they are transported to a sales line?
3. How many field processing methods do you know? What are they?
4. What is oil treating?
5. What is emulsion? How many types of emulsion do you know?
6. What's the function of a heater-treater?
7. What is a gun barrel?
8. What are the two types of storage tanks?
9. What is a separator?
10. What is a two-phase separator for? And a three-phase separator?
11. Why should we remove water from the oil or the natural gas? And how?
12. How many kinds of dehydrator do you know? What's their difference?

Unit 6

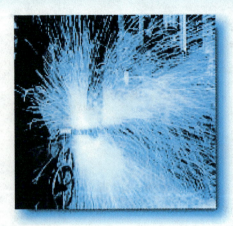

Welding Engineering
焊接工程

Look at the following terms involved in welding engineering. Do you know all of them? Could you add more?

- fusion welding
- pressure welding
- spot welding
- welding operation
- welding technology
- welding process
- welding sequence
- welding position
- welding speed
- welding stress
- SMAW
- FCAW
- GTAW

Now discuss the following questions with your partner. Please notice that some of the questions are open-ended.

1. What is welding?
2. How many welding methods do you know so far? And what are they?
3. Do you know the advantages of each welding method?

VOCABULARY ASSISTANT

fusion welding 熔接　　spot welding 点焊　　pressure welding 压接
welding process 焊接工艺　　welding sequence 焊接顺序　　welding technology 焊接技术
welding speed 焊接速度　　SMAW 焊条电弧焊　　GTAW 钨极氩弧焊
FCAW 自保护药芯焊丝半自动焊

Unit 6
Welding Engineering

AIMS

- Welding engineering and terms related to it

Part One　Word Power

Do you know the following terms related to welding engineering? Match them with their Chinese equivalents and learn them by heart.

Part A

A	B
1. fusion welding	A. 压接
2. welding position	B. 焊接工艺
3. spot welding	C. 焊接操作
4. welding process	D. 焊接速度
5. welding technology	E. 焊条电弧焊
6. welding sequence	F. 熔接
7. welding speed	G. 焊接应力
8. pressure welding	H. 点焊
9. welding operation	I. 钨极氩弧焊
10. welding stress	J. 焊接顺序
11. SMAW	K. 焊接位置
12. GTAW	L. 焊接技术

Part B

A	B
1. horizontal welding	A. 行走速度
2. vertical welding	B. 软钎焊
3. overhead welding	C. 电流安培
4. pass	D. 横焊
5. shielding gas	E. 送丝速度
6. voltage	F. 焊缝
7. power supply	G. 弧长
8. welding wire	H. 焊条
9. rivet	I. 硬钎焊
10. travel speed	J. 焊道
11. wire feed speed	K. 电压
12. preheat	L. 焊剂
13. ampere	M. 保护气体
14. arc length	N. 立焊
15. seam	O. 焊丝
16. welding flux	P. 极性
17. electrode	Q. 电源
18. soldering	R. 仰焊
19. braze	S. 铆钉
20. polarity	T. 预热

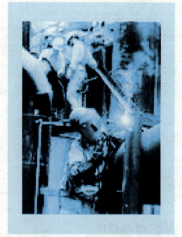

WELDING ENGINEERING UNIT 6

Look at these pictures, can you tell their names? And do you know their functions and how to use them?

Picture 1

Picture 2

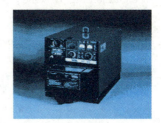

Picture 3

Picture 4

Picture 5

Picture 6

Picture 7

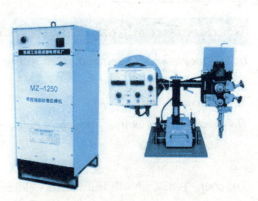

Picture 8

Part Two Listening

Listen to the passage about welding arc and fill in the missing words.

Passage 1

The welding ____1____ can be defined as a ____2____ group of electrical discharges that are formed and sustained by the ____3____ of a gaseous conduction medium. The ____4____ carriers for the gaseous medium are produced by thermal ____5____ and field emission. Many kinds of welding arcs have been conceived, each with a unique ____6____ in the field of metal joining. In some cases, the welding arc, an electrical discharge between two ____7____, is a steady state ____8____, but more frequently it is intermittent, subject to interruptions by an alternating directional ____9____ of current or by turbulent flow of the conducting gas ____10____.

VOCABULARY ASSISTANT

| discharge 放电 | sustain 维持 | thermal 热的 |
| conceive 构思 | intermittent 间歇的 | interruption 中断 |

Passage 2

____1____ is required for double-jointing, preparing ____2____ for crossings, mainline welding, tie-ins, and ____3____. Welding processes that are commonly used for pipeline ____4____ are gas submerged arc welding (restricted to double-jointing and fabrication), ____5____ metal arc welding (SMAW), or gas ____6____ arc welding (GMAW). Either a ____7____ welding technique or ____8____ welding may be used for ____9____ welding; manual welding is used for all other ____10____.

Part Three Dialogues

Read and act out the dialogues with your partners.

In the workshop, a teacher is showing some students around.

★ **Dialogue One**

The teacher is explaining some welding components about the internal welding machine to the students.

Teacher: Today, we will learn some welding **components**.
Student A: Welding components? What are they?

Teacher: Well, for example, *rotating ring hub assembly*.

Student B: What's its *function*?

Teacher: The unit supports, positions, and travels welding heads. Hub assembly supports rotating ring on roller bearings. Rotating ring supports the welding head at the rear by an anchor block and at front by vertical adjust assembly.

Student C: Is there a component called vertical adjust?

Teacher: Yes. And it supports front of welding head and assembly provides *vertical adjustment* of welding nozzle for correct contact tip-to-work distance.

Student B: Oh, I see.

Teacher: Who knows what the *service lead assembly* is?

Student A: Does the service lead contain a welding lead, gas tube, and wire feed motor connections?

Teacher: Yes, very good!

> **OCABULARY ASSISTANT**
>
> component 部件　function 作用
> rotating ring hub assembly 回转环形毂盘部件
> vertical adjust 垂直调整
> service lead assembly 服务线组件

Please answer the following questions after reading the dialogue.

1. What are they doing?
2. How many components have been mentioned? What are they?
3. What's the function of rotating ring hub assembly?
4. What's the function of vertical adjust?
5. What does the service lead assembly contain?

Please discuss with your partner about other components which you know.

★ **Dialogue Two**

Now the teacher is showing some tools, and the students are identifying what they are.

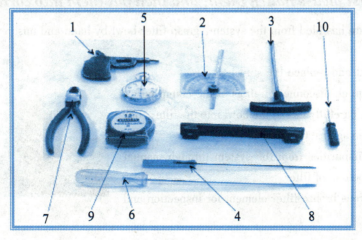

Teacher: Do you know the names of all the tools?
Student A: I know No. 2 is a protractor, and No. 5 is a stop watch.
Student B: No. 9 is a tape measure and No. 10 is a tweezers.
Teacher: Good! Others?
Student C: Is No. 3 a socket head driver, 5/32" Allen?
Student D: Yes, and No. 7 is wire cutters.
Teacher: Who knows what No.4 and No.6 are?
Student E: I know! No. 4, a cross screw driver, 1/8" Allen. And No. 6, screw drive, Common Slot W/Narrow Tip.
Student C: No. 1 is a feeler gauge, Tip-To Pipe Item one is fabricated from a welding tip with a homemade handle attached. And I also know tip diameter is used for gauging distance.
Teacher: Excellent! Of course, everybody knows No. 8 is a straight edge, magnetic base type.

Do you know all the names of the tools? If not, please learn by heart.

The following is a chart of typical mechanized welding spread. Please read it carefully and try to understand the process.

Typical Automated Welding Spread

The following is the process showing how air filters should be serviced regularly. First please match them, and then put them into correct order.

a. After all pressure has bled from the system, grasp filter bowl by hand and unscrew it from filter body.
b. Air-dry element and replace the stud bolt.
c. Uncouple the quick-disconnect fittings at the clamp nose.
d. After cleaning, carefully thread the bowl into the filter body and hand-tighten against O-ring seal.
e. Drain out the impurities from the system through manual drain cock at bottom of filter.
f. Remove the porous bronze filter element for inspection and cleaning.

g. Check whether the manual drain cock at the bottom of filter bowl is finger tight.

h. Wash the bronze filter elements in kerosene.

i. Clean filter bowl with kerosene moistened cloth and wipe dry.

j. Replace the baffle and tighten it hand-tight.

> A. 检查滤杯底部的手动旋气活塞是否拧紧。
> B. 清洗之后,仔细将滤杯旋进过滤器并手动拧紧O型密封圈。
> C. 吹干内部元件并更换柱头螺栓。
> D. 分开夹具前端的快速分离装置。
> E. 卸下多孔青铜过滤器元件进行检查和清洗。
> F. 在所有的气体压力从系统排出后,用手抓住滤杯并从过滤器由上旋下。
> G. 通过过滤器底部的手动排气旋塞排出系统内的杂质。
> H. 在煤油中清洗青铜过滤器。
> I. 用煤油浸湿的布擦拭滤杯并擦干。
> J. 更换挡板并只用手拧紧。

Discuss with your partners and translate the following sentences.

1. A whole welding process includes: striking the arc, welding, arc going out.
2. 现场焊接要注意安全。
3. There is plenty of poisonous gas in weld fume.
4. 为了防止焊条药皮受潮,焊条应放于干燥箱内。
5. Electrode consists of covering and core wire.
6. 请打开乙炔气瓶。
7. Welding power can be sorted into two types: alternated current welding machine and direct current welding machine.
8. 有防护白玻璃吗?
9. The polarity of power shall meet the process requirement.
10. 直流焊机分正接、反接。

VOCABULARY ASSISTANT

electrode 焊条   poisonous 有毒的
fume 烟尘   covering 药皮
alternated 交流的   process 工艺
polarity 极性   power 电源
dryer 干燥箱   damp 受潮
acetylene 乙炔

Use the correct form of the words from the box to complete the sentences and translate them.

| workshop | acid | weldablity | requirement | voltage | positive |

1. Carbon equivalent is a key parameter to evaluate the _____ of the material.
2. Straight polarity indicates the weldment connected to welding machine _____ polarity.
3. How much is the open-circuit _____ of the welding machine?
4. _____ electrode is not sensitive to iron rust.

5. Ventilation shall be good in the welding_____.
6. The welding material shall meet the_____.

Part Four Reading

Read the following passages and then answer the questions.

Passage 1
Part A

There are a number of methods of *joining* metal articles together, depending on the type of metal and the strength of the *joint* which is required. **Soldering** gives a satisfactory joint for light articles of steel, copper or brass, but the strength of a soldered joint is rather less than a joint which is brazed, *riveted* or welded. These methods of joining metal are normally adopted for strong permanent joints.

The simplest method of welding two pieces of metal together is known as pressure welding. The ends of metal are heated to a white heat—for iron, the welding temperature should be about 1300 °C—in a flame. At this temperature the metal becomes plastic. The ends are then pressed or hammered together, and the joint is smoothed off. Care must be taken to ensure that the surfaces are thoroughly cleaned first, for dirt will weaken the weld. Moreover, the heating of iron or steel to a high temperature causes oxidation, and a film of oxide is formed on the heated surfaces. For this reason, a *flux* is applied to the heated metal. At welding heat, the flux melts, and the

oxide particles are **dissolved** in it together with any other impurities which may be present. The metal surfaces are pressed together, and the flux is squeezed out from the center of the weld. A number of different types of weld may be used, but for fairly thick bars of metal, a V-shaped weld should normally be employed. It is rather strong than the ordinary **butt weld**.

Now please answer the following questions.

1. Before welding, why must the surface of metals be cleaned first?
2. What is the simplest method of welding two pieces of meals together?
3. What does it depend on when you want to join metal articles together?
4. What is the proper welding temperature for iron?
5. For a fairly thick bar of metal, why should a V-shaped weld be employed?

VOCABULARY ASSISTANT

join 接合点	joint 连接处,接缝	rivet 铆钉
dissolve 溶解	soldering 软钎焊	flux 助熔剂
butt weld 对焊	fusion 熔合,熔接	
oxyacetylene 氧乙炔气	torch 焊炬	constitute 构成
insulate 使绝缘,隔离	stainless 不锈的	

Part B

The heat for *fusion* welding is generated in several ways, depending on the sort of metal which is being welded and on its shape. An extremely hot flame can be produced from an *oxyacetylene torch*. For certain welds an electric arc is used. In this method, an electric current is passed across  two electrodes, and the metal surfaces are placed between them. The electrodes are sometimes made of carbon, but more frequently they are metallic. The work itself *constitutes* one of them and the other is an *insulated* filler rod. An arc is struck between the two, and the heat which is generated melts the metal at the weld. A different method, known as spot welding, is usually employed for welding sheets or plates of metal together. Spot welding requires both an electric current and a forging pressure to produce the weld. The two sheets to be spot welded are griped between copper electrodes through which a heavy current is passed; fusion occurs at the spots where the electrodes are thus applied. Metals with low electrical resistance will be difficult to be spot welded, whereas those with high resistance, such as *stainless* steel, will produce a spot weld readily.

Try to answer the two questions after reading the passage.

1. Will metals of low electric resistance be easy to spot weld?
2. When is spot welding used?

Passage 2

Weld ability is a much-used word, obviously intended to *describe* the ease—or otherwise with which a metal may be welded. Actually, there is no recognized method of *classifying* the weld ability of the different metals—there are too many variables. However, it is possible to attempt a brief *survey* of those *factors* which *affect* the weldability (for the fusion welding processes) of the most commonly used metals, that is, their thermal *characteristics*, and their reaction to the *application* of welding heat.

Generally, the factors which *decrease* the weldability, or increase the fusion welding difficulties of metals are:

1) Very high or very low heat *conductivity*
2) High degree of *expansion* when heated (high thermal expansion)
3) Low strength when hot (hot shortness)
4) Cold *brittleness* (cold shortness)
5) *Tendency* to oxidize readily when hot
6) Tendency for the weld to harden by air cooling or the quench effect of surrounding cold metal.

VOCABULARY ASSISTANT

weld ability 焊接性	describe 描述
classify 分类	survey 调查
factor 因素	affect 影响
characteristic 特点,特性	
application 应用	decrease 减少
conductivity 传导性	expansion 扩张
brittleness 脆	tendency 趋势

Now please answer the following questions.

1. What is the weldability of metals?
2. What are the factors that influence the weldability of metals?

Unit 7

Engineering Monitoring

工程监理

Look at the following terms involved in engineering monitoring. Do you know all of them? Could you add more?

Now discuss the following questions with your partner. Please notice that some of the questions are open-ended.

1. Do you know what the engineering monitoring is?
2. What kind of work does the supervisor do?
3. If you are a supervisor, what do you think is the most important factor?

> **VOCABULARY ASSISTANT**
>
> project 工程　supervision 监理　bid 投标　project manager 项目经理
> contractor 承包商　employer 业主　contract 合同　payment 支付
> quantity 数量　quality 质量　PM 项目管理　CM 建筑工程管理
> QHSE 质量、健康、安全、环境

Unit 7
Engineering Monitoring

AIMS

- Learn about welding engineering and terms related to it

Part One　Word Power

Do you know the following terms related to engineering monitoring? Match them with their Chinese equivalents and learn them by heart.

Part A

A	B
1. project	A. 合同
2. supervision	B. 数量
3. bid	C. 项目管理
4. project manager	D. 承包商
5. contractor	E. 支付
6. employer	F. 建筑工程管理
7. contract	G. 监理
8. payment	H. 质量
9. quantity	I. 工程
10. quality	J. 项目经理
11. PM	K. 业主
12. CM	L. 投标

Useful Sentences

1. The survey coordinator will plan and schedule the field survey operations in cooperation with the topographical survey.
   勘查协调员将结合地形勘查拟定和安排好现场勘查作业。
2. Field survey work and mapping will be supervised by the survey coordinator.
   现场勘查工作和制图工作均将接受勘查协调员的监督。
3. The design group is engaged in initial data organization now.
   设计组现已收集和整理原始资料。
4. All major changes will be documented for review and approval.
   所有主要变更将写成文件待审批。
5. The initial data will be ready in accordance with the contract.
   这些原始资料将按合同准备好。

Part B

A	B
1. project management	A. 财务
2. quality assurance and control	B. 项目管理
3. project control	C. 一个变压器站
4. planning and scheduling	D. 资产核销
5. cost control	E. 初步设计的审查
6. accounting	F. 一个污水池
7. capital construction (asset) auditing	G. 一个油泵房
8. project reporting	H. 项目控制
9. review of basic design	I. 项目报告
10. material inspection, testing	J. 一个停车棚
11. material transportation	K. 计划和进度

A	B
12. custom clearance	L. 质量保证和控制
13. unloading and storage at sites	M. 一个锅炉房
14. training for owner's personnel	N. 费用控制
15. boiler room	O. 清关
16. two fire water pool	P. 两个消防水池
17. transformer station	Q. 材料运输
18. a sewage controlling pool	R. 材料检验和测试
19. a carport	S. 为业主人员提供培训
20. an oil pump room	T. 现场的卸载和存储

Discuss with your partners and translate the following sentences.

1. 你有关于这个工程的参考资料吗？
2. Let's go and arrange this.
3. 请戴上安全帽。
4. Look out! Get out of the way.
5. 机器出现了故障。
6. Stop the machine and cut off the power.
7. 发动机怎么了？
8. We have finished this part of the process according to the plan.
9. 你知道如何调整这台新机器吗？
10. This equipment is supplied by the seller.

VOCABULARY ASSISTANT

arrange 安排　　cut off 切断
supply 提供　　process 工序
power 电源　　helmet 安全帽
reference materials 参考资料
engine 发动机　　adjust 调整

Useful Sentences

1. Contractor is to determine if sufficient and reliable electric power is available at site.
   承包商应确定现场的电源供给是否充足和可靠。
2. The battery system capacity shall be sized from min. 8 hours of backup power.
   电池系统容量最小应可容纳8小时的备用电池。
3. Confirm the switcher control power requirement and calculate battery size.
   确认开关装置的控制电源要求并计算电池的尺寸。

Use the correct form of the words from the box to complete the sentences and translate them.

characteristic　avert　risky　inspection　measures　completed　disassemble　satisfy

1. This is the equipment in _____ condition, that is the equipment fabricated at plant site.
2. Would you tell us the technical _____ about this project?

3. The result of the test run_____us.
4. We must avoid working in a_____way in violation of the rules.
5. We should lay down operating rules to_____accidents.
6. They have learnt how to_____and assemble the machines safely.
7. Strict safety_____must be taken so that we can finish the project successfully.
8. We have planned to finish the job of the_____equipment before Tuesday.

Useful Sentences

1. The owner will submit the bills of volume of work, estimate documentation and technical data without delay to the design company.
   业主将毫无拖延地提交工作量明细表、预算文件和技术数据。
2. The lack of supplementary, primary, prospecting and preliminary data may cause a delay in carrying out design work.
   缺少补充数据、原始数据、勘察初步数据可能使设计工作拖期完成。
3. The final data has been collected.
   最终资料已收全。
4. Does the apparatus (equipment, assembly tools, construction materials and insulating materials) correspond to the new norms and standards.
   机器(设备、装配工具、建筑材料、绝缘材料)是否符合新的规格和标准。

Part Two   Listening

Listen to the passage and fill in the missing words.

Passage 1

The_____1_____must be excavated in previously undisturbed soil so that the pipe is left on undisturbed soil. As an ____2____, side slopes may have the spoil, ditch line, and pipe on one ____3____, and the equipment on another. The ____4____ will grade so that conventional vehicles can travel along most of the ____5____. In steep, ragged terrain where this grading is not ____6____, it can be limited to the amount necessary to ____7____ the pipe, using towing ____8____ or winches. ____9____ are routed around these areas by using existing roads or constructing ____10____ roads near the site.

Listen again and try to understand the meaning of this passage.

Passage 2

Construction and building inspectors usually work alone. However, several may be assigned to large, complex ____1____, particularly because inspectors tend to specialize in different areas of ____2____. Though they spend considerable time inspecting construction ____3____, inspectors also spend time in a field office reviewing blueprints, answering letters or telephone calls, writing ____4____, and scheduling inspections.

Inspection sites are dirty and may be cluttered with tools, ____5____, or debris. Inspectors may have to climb ladders or many flights of stairs, or crawl around in tight spaces. Although their work ____6____ is not considered hazardous, inspectors, like other construction workers, wear hard hats and adhere to other safety ____7____ while at a construction site.

Inspectors normally work ____8____ hours. However, they may work additional hours during periods when a lot of construction is taking place. Also, if an accident ____9____ at a construction site, inspectors must respond immediately and may work additional hours to ____10____ their report.

VOCABULARY ASSISTANT

inspector 检查员 assign 指派
specialize 专攻 considerable 大量的
blueprint 蓝图,详细的计划 schedule 安排
debris 瓦砾 hazardous 危险的
additional 额外的 respond 回复

ENGINEERING MONITORING UNIT 7

Listen again and try to find out the work of the inspectors.

Useful Sentences

1. Due to defective equipment or dated equipment they must be replaced.
   由于设备有缺陷或陈旧,必须予以更换。
2. Bear responsibility for the quality of equipment and observance of the schedule of erection work.
   对设备质量和安装工作进度负责。
3. Assist the owner in development of training programs and manuals.
   协助业主编写培训程序和手册。
4. The detection and alarm system of the flammable gas is to be installed at the process installation area of each station plant for the gas compression, stations, sub-transmission stations, pipe pigging station and branch (trunk) line stations.
   压气站、分输站、清管站和支(干)线各场站的工艺装置区均应设置可燃气体检测和报警系统。

Passage 3

The ___1___ of the HSE chief ___2___ of the CST Headquarters Office

- Organize to work out the ___3___ supervision plan and the detailed rules for the ___4___ for the CST Headquarters Office;
- Organize to ___5___ the environment supervision plan and the detailed rules for the implementation by the CST Site Offices;
- Guide and supervise ___6___ environment supervision ___7___ in the CST Headquarters Office as well as the implementation of the work done by each CST Site Office;
- Organize to ___8___ examination of relevant environment supervision personnel in both the CST Headquarters Office and the Site Offices;
- Advise or make ___9___ regarding the environment protection work of WEPP;
- Report to the HSE chief supervisor about issues relating to environment protection in WEPP and accept ___10___ from the chief supervisor.

VOCABULARY ASSISTANT

HSE 健康,安全,环保　　detailed 详细的
CST Headquarters Office 工程监理总部
implementation 实施　　WEPP 西气东输工程

After listening, think about the two questions.

1. What does HSE stand for?
2. Do you know the full name of CST and WEPP?

If you have finished the listening exercise, try to translate Passage One into Chinese. And then compare your translation with the reference answer.

管沟必须在土壤扰动之前开挖,以便钢管搁置在未扰动的土上。斜坡面可能有泥石、沟线,可以选择钢管在一个平面,而设备在另一个平面。承包商采取措施定坡降线,确保常用的车辆能沿多数施工作业带通行。在陡峭、粗糙的地方,无法进行定坡降线,这将限制安装钢管必须使用牵引设备和绞车。在这些区段,车辆只能沿着现有的道路或在现场临时修建的道路通行。

Part Three　Dialogues

★ Dialogue One
● In the work site

> **VOCABULARY ASSISTANT**
>
> centrifugal compressor 离心式压缩机
> install 安装
> flow diagram 流程图
> phenomenon 现象
> Safety First 安全第一

Mr Li: Welcome to our work site. I am in charge of this section. This is a plot plan **flow diagram**. Please show us how to do it.
Mr Zhang: How many man-days do you need?
Mr Li: This project will take five thousand man-days to complete.
Mr Zhang: How is everything with this project?
Mr Li: The project is making good progress. The new **centrifugal compressor** will be **installed** next week.
Mr Zhang: We should increase efficiency and shorten the time limit for project but pay more attention to safe operation.

Please act the dialogue with your partner.

Try to answer the following questions.

1. Who is in charge of this section?
2. How many labours do they need?
3. Does everything go well?
4. When will they install the new centrifugal compressor?

★ Dialogue Two
● About safety

A: We would like to know your opinion about site work.
B: First, I think you must ensure that your workers wear safety helmet.
A: Yes, workers must know "Safety First" by heart, this is very important.

B: Second, ask them not to drop cigarette ends about. It's very dangerous.

A: I also notice this **phenomenon** must be stopped.

B: I find that some of your workers are not so skilled as required. I suggest that on-site training be necessary for your project.

A: Yes, I agree, some training will fit them for the job. Thank you very much for your advice.

> *After reading the dialogue, what do you know about safety in the work site?*
> *Can you think of other things we should pay attention to for safety?*
> *Try to make similar dialogues with your partner.*

Useful Sentences
No Smoking. 禁止吸烟。   No Photography. 禁止拍照。
No Parking. 禁止停车。   Exit. 出口。
No Thoroughfare. 禁止通行。（此路不通）
Emergency Exit. 紧急出口。
Keep Away! Danger! 请勿靠近！危险！
Look Out! 小心！

Part Four   Reading

Passage 1

Inspectors are used to monitor and **enforce** the following:

- **Topsoil** or grade spoil is not placed on uncleared ground.
- Cuts and spoil storage piles are sloped for **stability** and do not present a hazard for the public, livestock, or wildlife, and they are fully contained within the boundaries of the right-of-way or **temporary** workspace.
- Topsoil is placed in such a way that mixing with spoil will not occur.
- Soil is not placed in streams; bridges or **culverts** are used where it is necessary to maintain **drainage** in streams.
- Land-use agreements are obtained and approved prior to grading temporary **access** trails.
- Final right-of-way **profile** will allow the pipe to be bent and laid in undisturbed soil in accordance with **specifications**.
- Valve and meter station sites are graded level to the **elevation** specified on the construction drawings. Where cuts and fills are required, site boundaries must be adequately marked and **staked** to ensure that the final elevation is as specified by the contractor's surveyors.

- Where **blasting** is required, provision is made to ensure loose rock does not scatter over the right-of-way or **adjacent** land, causing damage to property or risk to workers and the public. The inspector should have the contractor pick up and **dispose** of any fly-rock. Mats or earth cover should be used in the vicinity of highways, houses, etc.
- The contractor has obtained all the required permits for the use of **explosives**, and met the terms of these permits. Only qualified drilling and blasting personnel are employed in the blasting operation.
- Proper **notification** is given to landowners and the public prior to blasting.
- All blasting materials are stored in an approved magazine.

VOCABULARY ASSISTANT

enforce 执行　　topsoil 表层土　　stability 稳定性　　temporary 临时的
culvert 阴沟　　drainage 排水　　access 进入　　explosive 炸药
specification 规格　　elevation 海拔　　blast 炸开　　profile 外形
adjacent 附近的　　dispose 处理　　stake 用木桩支撑
notification 通知

Please identify the following statements are true or false.

1. Topsoil is placed on uncleared ground.
2. Cuts and spoil storage piles are fully contained within the boundaries of the right-of-way or temporary workspace.
3. In the place where it is necessary to maintain drainage in streams bridges or culverts are used.
4. The pipe can't be bent for the final right-of-way profile.
5. If the contractor needs to use explosives, he must ask for permission.

Now think about the following questions.

6. The place where cuts and fills are required, is it necessary that the site boundaries must be adequately marked and staked? Why?
7. How to avoid damage to property or risk to workers and the public when blasting is necessary?
8. Is there any requirement for the people in the blasting operation?

Passage 2

Inspectors will ***monitor*** to ensure that pipe is being handled so as to avoid damage to the pipe and coating, that all ***parameters*** specified by the welding procedure are being met, and that all welders are qualified, internal lineup ***clamps*** are not released until the stringer bead is complete. Welds are marked with welders' numbers, ***longitudinal seams*** are correctly located, and pipe coating is protected from weld ***spatter*** damage. Weather conditions are acceptable for welding. Two welding passes are completed on all welds at the end of each day.

Welds that are to be left for more than 48 hours have one ***mechanized*** fill ***pass*** or two ***manual*** fill passes completed. All open ends of welded sections are securely night-capped at the end of each day, no waste material or debris, such as welding rod ***stubs***, is left on the right-of-way or placed in the pipeline ***trench***. All welds found to be unacceptable by nondestructive testing are cut out and replaced or repaired using a qualified procedure; gaps that are left in the right-of-way are necessary for landowners, livestock/wildlife.

VOCABULARY ASSISTANT

monitor 检查　　parameter 参数
clamp 夹钳　　　longitudinal 纵向的
seam 焊缝　　　mechanized 机械的
spatter 飞溅　　manual 手工的
stub 残片　　　trench 沟　　pass 焊道

Now think about the following questions.

1. When can the internal lineup clamps be released?
2. Are weather conditions acceptable for welding?

Unit 8

HSE

健康、安全、环保

Look through the following words and phrases concerned with HSE. Do you know all of them?

disposable devices   dispensary   diarrhea

allergic rhinitis   dental care

safety helmet   safety netting   discharging rod

air strainer   water strainer

safety switch   do not cast   stretcher

antibiotics   to ease the itching and burning

Now answer the following questions.

1. Do you know HSE, what do the three letters stand for separately?
2. Could you add more words or phrases related to HSE?
3. According to your understanding, which one is the most important among Healthy, Safety and Environment?

VOCABULARY ASSISTANT

disposable devices 一次性使用器具　　dispensary 医护室　　diarrhea 腹泻
allergic rhinitis 过敏鼻炎　　　　　　safety helmet 安全帽　　safety net 安全网
discharging rod 避雷针　　　　　　　air strainer 空气过滤器　water strainer 滤水器
antibiotics 抗生素　　stretcher 担架　　to ease the itching and burning 止痒,减轻灼伤

AIM

- Know about knowledge concerned with HSE.

Unit 8
HSE

Part One　Word Power

Find the definition in Column B which matches the words or expressions in Column A.

A	B
1. Put on your (safety) helmet.	A. 穿好救生衣。
2. That's against the rule.	B. 这是违章作业。
3. Have your BA (breathing apparatus) near you!	C. 严禁使用明火!
4. Put on life jacket!	D. 我眼睛痛。
5. It's a high voltage area here.	E. 消暑解热,明目怡神。
6. Open flame is strictly prohibited!	F. 带上安全帽。
7. Don't overrun your equipment.	G. 保证附近有防毒面具。
8. Go and get a stretcher here, quickly!	H. 快把担架拿来!
9. He got malaria.	I. 这是高压区。
10. I have a sore eye.	J. 这里危险,不要站人。
11. It's an infectious disease.	K. 驻工地总代表。
12. It is dangerous, keep away please.	L. 他需要输两天液。
13. Relieving heat and sunstroke, refreshing and beneficial to the eyes.	M. 他得了疟疾。
14. Tell the base to get a chopper here.	N. 有人受伤,快叫医生!
15. Someone has got injured, call the medic, and hurry up!	O. 有人落水!
16. Man overboard!	P. 通知基地派飞机来。
17. Sorry, drinking liquor is not allowed on the rig.	Q. 要点火啦,快开消防泵!
18. The oil will soon be set ablaze. Start the fire pumps right now!	R. 这种疾病传染!
19. He needs intravenous drip for two days.	S. 对不起,平台上不准喝酒。
20. Resident construction manager.	T. 不要超负荷运转。

Part Two Listening

Listen to the following passage about mental health carefully and try to fill in the blanks.

Keeping Pleasant

On construction site, weighed down with _____1_____ and pressure from the realities of their work, many project managers, controller staff members, engineers and workers have lost their sense of humor. They tend to keep a _____2_____ face all day long and fail to keep life in _____3_____. They almost forget how to smile. Well there goes a saying, "Laugh, and grow fat." Laughter _____4_____ tension, and smiling helps create a pleasant social atmosphere. Thus, in a way, a sense of humor is an elixir that helps cure mental diseases. Some doctors suggest that the staff engaged in the projects can improve their _____5_____ and mental health by reading humorous stories or watching funny movies. This proves that a sense of humor helps them look at the world in a true and healthy light and makes their life worth living.

> **VOCABULARY ASSISTANT**
>
> controller 管理员
> Laugh, and grow fat 心宽体胖
> elixir 万灵丹

Listen to the following dialogue about check-up carefully (3 times) and try to fill in the blanks.

A: Dr. Hawkins   B: Mr. Smith

H: Hi, Mr. Smith. _____1_____ are you here today?

S: I think it _____2_____ be a good idea to _____3_____ a check-up.

H: Yes, well you haven't _____4_____ one for...five years. You should have one every year.

S: I know. I _____5_____ as long as there's nothing wrong, why _____6_____ the doctor?

H: Well, the best way to avoid _____7_____ is to find out about them early. So, try to come _____8_____ once a year for your _____9_____.

S: O.K.

H: Let me see here. Your eyes and ears look fine. Take a _____10_____, please. Do you smoke, Mr. Smith?

S: Yes.

H: Smoking is the _____11_____ cause of _____12_____ and heart disease, you know. You really should _____13_____.

S: I've tried a hundred times, but I just can't seem to _____14_____ the habit.

H: Well, we have _____15_____ and some medicines that might help. I'll give you more information before you leave.

S: O.K., thanks, doctor.

Listen to the dialogue between Human Resources Manager (HR) and Company President (CP) and then fill in the blanks.

HR: As a reasonably large company, we are required to produce a written ____1____ policy.
CP: Have you got a ____2____ for me to look at?
HR: No, we are still doing the risk assessment for the main office building.
CP: Well this is a brand-new office facility, it must be one of the safest places to work in the whole Langfang city.
HR: Yes, but you'd be surprised at all the ways that people can find to hurt themselves!
CP: I know. So what about ____3____ ?
HR: Well our foreign employees will be covered by their own insurance.
CP: And what about the Chinese employees?
HR: We are going to have to take out ____4____ cover for them. We are waiting for some quotes now.
CP: Won't the insurance companies come and inspect the ____5____ ?
HR: Yes, they want to come round before finalizing any ____6____ of cover.
CP: We will just have to make sure that everything is completely satisfactory.
HR: The manager has been making all the preparations. There shouldn't be a problem.
CP: OK. I'd better give him a call after this and make sure he has everything under control.
HR: The other thing I want to say is the ____7____ program we are planning to launch.
CP: Sounds like a good idea. What do you have in mind?
HR: It is expected to have one proper ____8____ facility for each floor in the office building.
CP: So do we have to offer training program if we don't have enough qualified people?
HR: Yes, but it doesn't cost very much to get people ____9____ .
CP: Great. Hopefully we'll get plenty of ____10____ then.

> **VOCABULARY ASSISTANT**
> assessment 估价,评价额   insurance 保险   inspect 检查
> premises (法律)前述事项   fort 要点   qualified 合格的

Read again and answer the following questions.

1. What should the leader do if he works in a reasonably large company?
2. What kind of people will be covered by their own insurance?
3. What are they planning to launch?

Look at these pictures, can you tell all kinds of foods mentioned in the picture? Work with your partner and tell your favorites in each picture. Could you add any other foods which are good for your body?

Discuss with your partners and translate the jokes.

If you are on a boring and dull construction site, what will you do? How to make you and your colleagues pleasant?

Joke

1. Vegetarianism

A man was talking to his friends about why he was a vegetarian. "I'm not a vegetarian because I love animals," he said, "I'm a vegetarian because I hate plants!"

2. Swiss roll

Question: How do you make a Swiss roll?

Answer: You push them down the Alps.

3. Balance diet

Question: What is a balance diet?

Answer: The same amount of cookies in each hand!

Part Three Dialogues

★ **Dialogue One**

● **Seeing a doctor**

Doctor: What's wrong with you?

Patient: My head hurts badly.

Doctor: How long has it been like this?
Patient: Since last night.
Doctor: Do you have a sleeping problem?
Patient: Yes, I even can't fall asleep these days.
Doctor: I think you'd better have a further examine, and before the result comes out, try to relax yourself and take the medicine before you sleep. It will help you to kill the pain and make you sleep well.

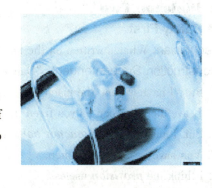

Patient: Is it serious, Doctor?
Doctor: When the result comes out, I will tell you about it. Remember, never be afraid or be too tired.
Patient: Ok, thank you, Doctor.

Read the above dialogue carefully and make up short dialogues by reference to the useful words and expressions in the boxes below.

USEFUL WORDS

toothache   how often   brush one's teeth   candies   not good for   twice a day or three times a day   will be better than now

Useful Expressions

He feels headache, nausea and vomiting. (他觉得头痛、恶心和想吐。)
He feels light-headed. (他觉得头晕。)
His eyes feel itchy and he has been sneezing. (他眼睛发痒, 而且一直在打喷嚏。)
He has bouts of uncontrollable coughing. (他一阵阵地咳嗽, 难以控制。)
He is short of breath, even when he has not been exercising, he is breathless. (他气短, 即使不运动, 他也是上气不接下气。)
It is not serious. 病情不严重。
You need a thorough examination. 你需要做一个全面检查。
You can carry on with your work. 可以继续工作。
Feeling well again is a rather slow process, I'm afraid. 恐怕痊愈将是一个很慢的过程。
Please show your tongue. 请伸出舌头。
Please lie on your back (stomach, right side, left side). 请仰卧(俯卧、右侧卧、左侧卧)。

★ Dialogue Two
● Safety First

Technician: What's written on the boom side?

Construction Superintendent: "Danger! Keep away from under boom!"

T: But, I have to rope the machine.

C: Leave there as soon as you fixed it.

T: But, I must *guide* the *anchor bolts* in.

C: You have to take a risk then.

T: I think the *provision* useless.

C: No, it isn't. It tells you to keep safety in mind all the time.

T: Yes, I agree, "Safety first."

C: Have you ever seen things dropping down from the hoist height?

T: No, never.

C: That's what used to happen.

T: Really?

C: Why not! Especially small things like bricks and so on, and *breaking rope* or *dropping boom* happened sometimes.

T: Thank you! I will keep that in mind. I'd better wear my safety helmet.

VOCABULARY ASSISTANT

technician 技术员　　construction superintendent 工地主任
guide 导入　　　　　anchor bolts 地脚螺栓
provision 条文　　　breaking rope 断绳
dropping boom 掉臂

★ Dialogue Three
● An Accident

Supervisor: Oh! There must be something the matter!

Controller staff member: The *crane* turned over.

S: Anybody wounded!

C: One died and several wounded.

S: Have you been there?

C: When I was watching at the *hook block*, the accident happened.

S: How far were you staying?

C: Not far. I was standing by the side of the crane, but escaped in time.

S: It was really a danger.

C: The operator was a young man, he died.

S: Did they break the crane?

C: Of course. The boom was broken and **work schedule** must be changed for a new one.
S: The must be postponed then.
C: And, it **costs** a lot of money as well.

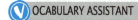OCABULARY ASSISTANT

supervisor 检查员   controller staff member 管理员
crane 起重机   hook block 吊钩
work schedule 工作计划   cost 损失

★ **Dialogue Four**
● **Emergency**

Foreman: Look, Jim. That man just fell down over there.
Safety coordinator: We'd better see if he's O.K.
Foreman: Sir...sir? Are you all right? Sir?
Safety coordinator: He's not answering. You'd better check his pulse and breathing.
Foreman: Oh, no. He's not breathing, and there's no **pulse**. Call 120.
Safety coordinator: Hello? Yes. Someone has passed out near the job site. He isn't breathing and does not have a pulse. Yes. My colleague is performing **CPR**. OK. Thank you. They're sending an **ambulance**. Here, let me help.

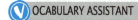OCABULARY ASSISTANT

foreman 工长   safety coordinator 安全协调员
pulse 脉搏,脉的一次跳动
CPR=cardiopulmonary resuscitation [医]心肺复苏法   ambulance 救护车

Read the above three dialogues carefully and translate the third one. Answer the following questions, and then make up a short dialogue with your partner to fit the following situation.

(1) Before entering a construction site, what should be done first?
(2) When facing a sudden accident, what will you do? What character should you have?

Use the correct form of the words from the box to complete the sentences and translate them.

engine	updated	switchboard	procedure	belt	insulated

1. The station bills need to be_____.
2. Wear and secure your safety_____when you work above the deck.
3. Provide two independent means to start the emergency generator_____.
4. Clean the internals of the emergency_____.
5. Our electrical tools are double_____and approved to international safety standards.
6. Safety_____shall be followed at all the times.

Part Four Reading

Grasp the Structure of Safety Agreement and know the items clearly.

Passage 1

Safety Agreement

Project Owner (Full name)
Contractor (Full name)
This safety agreement is signed based on "*Safety Production Law of People's Republic of China,*" "*Construction Law of People's Republic of China*" and other relevant legal requirements.

Safety Agreement

Contracted Work Description:
Contracted Work Name:
Contracted Work Location:
Contracted Work Content:
Funding Resource:
Scope of Contracted Work:

Contract Duration:
Commencement Date:
Commissioning Date:
Total Days:

Agreement ensure specification and work safety, engineering design and working method must comply with national safety legal requirements and standards. Contractor also must comply with Site Safety Management Requirements of ***West-East Gas Pipeline Project***:

a. Attachment C—"Construction, HSE & Security Rules" and

b. Attachment J—"Project HSE-Security ***Discipline*** Procedure."

Safety System shall be implemented and safety management shall be reinforced within the scope of contracted work; effective measures shall be taken to prevent incidents from occurring. A full-time safety coordinator shall be hired for every 50 workers within the contracted work.

Contractor's responsibility for Health, Safety, Environmental and Security compliance at the worksite within the scope of contracted work is assigned to the following persons: (in case of change of the persons, contractor must formally inform project owner by submitting documented notice.)

Project Manager: (Name)

Safety Coordinator: (Name)

Contractor must take full safety responsibilities for the contracted work, and the legal representative of the contractor has safety responsibility for its company. Contractor shall take all of the legal responsibilities for the property damage or personal harm (including project owner, contractor itself, or the 3rd party) from the incidents caused by its employees (including temporary employees).

Safety Agreement

If any lawsuit, arbitration or other proceeding involving a claim related to such safety accidents, whatever it is based on contract or infringement, civil laws or administrative rule, is threatened or instituted against project owner and/or any other third parties, the liable contractor shall give full cooperation in the defense of such proceedings. The ***liable*** contractor shall ***indemnify*** project owner and any of the third parties and hold them harmless against any damages or other compensation pursuant to a valid judgment issued by a court or ***arbitration*** body of competent jurisdiction with respect to such claim.

Contractor should fully consider of direct or indirect management fee for site safety, security, health, and environmental, including providing personal protective equipments, safety equipment, improving work condition safety, and etc. Budget allocated for safety expenses cannot be used for any other purposes.

Safety training system must be established, and contractor has responsibility for providing its employees with safety trainings. Operators cannot perform their task without completing safety training. The purpose of HSE Induction provided by Project owner is to explain West-East Gas Pipeline Project site safety rules. Contractor is still legally responsible for the safety trainings required within contractor itself.

Contractor must make sure security and first-aid provided within the contracted work scope to protect its own property and people safety within the scope of contracted work.

Contractor has safety responsibility for the sub-contractors within the contracted work scope. Contractor should supervise sub-contractor workers' work and sign safety agreement with sub-contractors. A copy of the safety agreement should be kept on-site.

Project Owner (Stamp)

Contractor (Stamp)

Address

Legal Representative

Deputy

Telephone

Fax Number

VOCABULARY ASSISTANT

Safety Production Law of People's Republic of China 《中华人民共和国安全生产法》
Construction Law of People's Republic of China 《中华人民共和国建筑法》
West-East Gas Pipeline Project 西气东输项目
discipline 纪律   liable 有责任的   indemnify 赔偿,保障
arbitration 仲裁,裁定

Grasp the main idea. Try your best to comprehend the commit.

Passage 2

Our HSE Commitment

CNPC has always believed that people and the environment are our two most important resources. Therefore, it is one of our top concerns to protect the environment and safeguard the health and safety of our staff.

We are committed to:

Obeying the laws and *regulations* of the countries where we *operate* and fully respect local customs.

Attaching utmost importance to safety and taking *adequate* precautions.

Protecting the environment by promoting clean operations and the rational use of resources.

Optimizing the **allocation** of our HSE resources and continuously improving our HSE management.

Appointing the chief executive of each *subsidiary* as the person with the greatest responsibility for HSE and taking HSE performance as a key *criterion* for rewards and *penalties*, as well as *recruitment* and *subcontracting*.

Reinforcing HSE training to establish and maintain an excellent HSE culture.

Complete honesty and openness with the public regarding our HSE performance.

Consistency in our HSE concepts wherever we are and in all sectors of our business.

Our HSE Concepts

Giving priority to people, safety and environment.

Accidents are controllable and avoidable.

HSE performance is determined by responsibility, design quality, and prevention.

Our HSE Objectives

Zero accidents, zero injuries and zero pollution to achieve a world-class HSE performance.

VOCABULARY ASSISTANT

regulation 法规	operate 操作,执行	attach 附加
utmost 最高的	adequate 足够的	optimize 尽量有效地利用
allocation 分配	subsidiary 附属人员	criterion 判断准则
penalty 惩罚	recruitment 休养	subcontract 续签合同
reinforce 加强	consistency 言行一致	

Part Five   Case Study

Environmental Protection in the West-East Gas Pipeline Project

Since the project became fully operational in 2005, it has benefited over 200 million people. It plays an important role in adjusting our energy structure, coping with energy shortages in Central and Eastern China, especially in the Yangtze River Delta, promoting economic development, improving air quality, raising residents' living standards and promoting the saving of resources and measures to protect the environment.

The project spans the four valleys of the Yellow River, the Huaihe River, the Yangtze River and the Taihu Lake. It crosses the *terrain*, deserts, *arid* and semi-arid regions of the Gobi Desert, as well as the *loess plateaus*, grasslands, woodlands and mountainous areas of Shanxi and Henan provinces. It also travels farmland in the Yellow River-Huaihe Plain and the Yangtze-Huaihe Plain, as well as a network of rivers. There are 143 micro-ecological areas, four national parks, one national ecological reserve, four environmentally sensitive areas and many places of historic importance along the trunk line of nearly 4,000 kilometers. The project was complicated by various types of water loss and *erosion* in and along the pipeline.

To protect the environment and prevent water loss and soil erosion in these adverse and environmentally sensitive sections, *gravel* covering was applied to the Gobi Desert areas, while large-scale artificial meadows were transplanted in the grasslands affected by wind and sandstorms. In addition, comprehensive engineering and biological measures were combined to improve the conditions of the loess plateaus, as well as hilly and mountainous areas. On the plains, farmlands were returned to production and riverbanks were *consolidated*.

During the construction of the pipeline, a *detour* strategy was adopted to avoid damaging natural reserves and places of historic significance, as well as other sensitive areas. According to the original plan, the pipeline had to cut across the *buffer zone* of the Alkin Wild Camel Nature Reserve for about 100 kilometers. Following our environmental impact studies, we decided to shift the pipeline away from the buffer zone, which added nearly 200 million *yuan* to the budget. It was to protect rare wild animals and to minimize the negative impact on the environment.

Our pipeline crosses ancient sections of the Great Wall 12 times. Ceiling-crossing technologies ensured these historic relics were undamaged.

After the completion of the project, a national examination indicated that all environmental protection measures had been well *implemented* during the construction and commissioning period of the pipeline. All *pollutant* discharges, as well as water and soil conservation measures, have satisfied both local and national standards.

As a result, the West-East Gas Pipeline Project was awarded the title of "National Environmentally Friendly Project."

VOCABULARY ASSISTANT

terrain 地带,地域
plateaus 高原(pl. plateaux)
consolidate 巩固
implement 工具,手段
arid 干燥的
erosion 侵蚀,腐蚀
detour 便道,迂路
pollutant 污染物质
loess (地理)黄土
gravel 碎石,沙石
buffer zone 缓冲地带

Fill in the blanks according to the passage.

1. It also travels farmland in the Yellow River-Huaihe Plain and the Yangtze-Huaihe Plain, as well as a _____ of rivers.
2. We decided to shift the pipeline away from the buffer zone, which added nearly 200 million **Yuan** to the _____.
3. While large-scale _____ meadows were transplanted in the grasslands affected by wind and sandstorms.
4. A national examination indicated that all environmental protection _____ had been well implemented during the construction and commissioning period of the pipeline.
5. It plays an important role in adjusting our energy structure, coping with energy shortages in Central and Eastern China, especially in the Yangtze River _____.
6. The West-East Gas Pipeline Project was _____ the title of "National Environmentally Friendly Project."
7. During the construction of the pipeline, a detour strategy was adopted to avoid damaging natural reserves and places of historic significance, as well as other _____ areas.
8. _____ technologies ensured these historic relics were undamaged.
9. The project spans the _____ valleys of the Yellow River, Huaihe River, Yangtze River and Taihu Lake.

Talk about your feelings with your partner, in your opinion, what is the most important thing among environment, interest, the process of the project and the reputation of enterprise?

Unit 9

Engineering Maintaining and Repairing

工程维修

Study the following words and phrases concerned with engineering maintaining and repairing. Do you know all of them?

- pig
- repair worker
- repair over again
- cleaning
- hacksaw
- chisel
- socket
- wrench
- hook spanner
- adjustable wrench
- pipe wrench
- ratchet wrench
- open end wrench
- screw driver
- hand vice
- pliers

Now answer the questions.

1. Do you know anything about engineering maintaining and repairing?
2. Can you add more words related to tools?

VOCABULARY ASSISTANT

repair worker 维修工 to repair over again 返修 cleaning 洗油,去油,清洗
hammer (hacksaw, chisel, socket, wrench, hook spanner, adjustable wrench, pipe wrench, ratchet wrench, open end wrench, screw driver, hand vice, pliers) 手锤(钢锯、凿子、套筒扳手、钩扳手、活动扳手、管扳手、棘轮扳手、开口扳手、螺丝刀、手钳、扁嘴钳)

Unit 9
Engineering Maintaining and Repairing

AIM
- Know about knowledge concerned with engineering maintaining and repairing

Part One Word Power

Find the definition in Column B that matches the words or expressions in Column A.

A	B
1. MPI the brake linkage system.	A. 打开防喷器闸板进行内部检查。
2. Determine the origin of the air leak and rectify this.	B. 调整安全阀。
3. Renew brake rim because of excessive wear.	C. 用大锤打。
4. Measure the master bushings for wear.	D. 找出漏气的地方并处理。
5. Have BOP ram opened up for internal inspection.	E. 测量主补芯磨损情况。
6. Strike it with a sledge hammer.	F. 对刹车连接系统进行磁粉探伤。
7. Maintain the hoisting system.	G. 这台离合器打滑需修理。
8. This clutch needs repairing.	H. 更换磨损严重的刹车鼓。
9. Regulate the relief valve.	I. 这台离合器需要修理。
10. This clutch needs repairing due to it slipping.	J. 快找仪表工来检查一下。

A	B
11. Clean the hydraulic oil filter.	K. 1号泵有点毛病,请用2号泵。
12. Take off all the valve caps and check for the problem.	L. 快速放气阀有一点毛病。
13. Fetch the instrument man to check it quickly.	M. 检查和保养一下游动系统。
14. The mud pump is O.K.?	N. 泥浆泵有问题没有?
15. The NO.1 rig pump is out of order. Use the NO.2 Please.	O. 保养提升系统。
16. This bolt needs renewing because the thread is stripped.	P. 清洗一下液压油滤清器。
17. There's something wrong with the quick-discharge air valve.	Q. 拆开所有凡尔盖检查。
18. Determine the origin of the air leak and rectify this.	R. 需要一把三角锉刀。
19. We want a triangle file.	S. 找出漏气的地方并处理。
20. Check and maintain the hoisting system.	T. 这个螺丝滑扣了,要换一个新的。

Part Two Listening

Listen to the following passage about HOT-TAPPING AND PLUGGING three times and try to fill in the blanks. Grasp the main idea of the two items.

Item 1

Hot-tapping and Plugging Object and Significance

Pipeline hot-tapping and _____1_____ operation is a _____2_____ and _____3_____ repairing technique for operating pipelines which features safe, environment protection, economic, high efficiency, also suits pipeline maintenance, rehabilitation, _____4_____ repair for sudden accident (such as emergency repair under pressure, replace the corroded _____5_____ sections, fix additional devices and _____6_____ transformation etc.) The pipeline medium can be crude oil, product oil, chemicals, natural gas etc.

Item 2

Economic Profit Analysis of Hot-tapping and Plugging

The past conventional method was to _____7_____ or even empty the pipeline before maintenance and repairs, or some temporary remedy measures _____8_____ which brought about hidden dangers to pipeline safety, and also the economic loss. The _____9_____ technique can solve the problems quickly, safely without _____10_____ of pipeline production.

VOCABULARY ASSISTANT

hot-tapping and plugging 带压开孔、封堵   pipeline 管道   rehabilitation 治疗,改造
emergency 突发事故   corroded 腐蚀的 remedy 补救

Useful Expressions

maintenance and emergency repairing technique 维抢修技术
repair under pressure 带压抢修
fix additional devices 加装装置
off-take pipeline 分输改造
crude oil 原油
product oil 成品油
natural gas 天然气

Listen to the following passage about process of tank mechanical washing three times and try to fill in the blanks. Grasp the main idea of the two items.

Item 1

Process of Tank Mechanical Washing

Crude oil _____1_____ washing equipment mainly consists of: extraction and suction system for crude oil _____2_____ and transferring, heat exchanging system, oil supplying system for supplying washing medium, washer, nitrogen, gas monitoring system, oil/water separating system and _____3_____ piping and fittings etc.

Tank washing process is that the washer _____4_____ washing medium onto washing surfaces at certain temperature, pressure and _____5_____ rate to remove the _____6_____ from washing surfaces, recover and treat the oil.

Item 2

Medium of Tank Mechanical Washing

Washing medium may be _____7_____ oil or the same type of medium. Hot water as a washing medium shall be used after "wash oil with oil" as crude oil consists of light _____8_____ i.e. solvent component which speed up the dissolution of deposits. Deposits and washing medium shall be mixed, then be _____9_____ and finally be transferred to recovery tank.

Crude oil washing equipment, washing tank and recovery tank are connected with process piping and form a washing _____10_____ system. The circulating washing is achieved through the flow of thin oil.

VOCABULARY ASSISTANT

medium 介质,手段   suction 抽吸   condensate 凝结物

Use the correct form of the words from the box to complete the passage and translate it.

| pollution | affect | seen | within | cleaned | without | recovery | hidden |

Features of Mechanical Washing Technique

- High crude oil ___1___ rate: over 98%.
- Indirect heating with steam, not ___2___ physical property of crude oil.
- High deposited (over 2m high) tank can be ___3___ while manual cleaning shall be impossible.
- Utilizing crude oil as cleaning medium at certain temperature, pressure and flow rate, metal color can be ___4___ on the washing surface.
- Short tank washing period with high efficiency, ___5___ influence of the weather condition, cannot affect the cleaning operation and thus operation period can be ensured.
- Safety is guaranteed, the concentration of oxygen and flammable gas in the tank can be controlled by nitrogen and the ___6___ danger caused by static is avoided.
- Friendly cleaning atmosphere, without environment ___7___. Oil/water separating process may recover the reusable oil and the washing water can meet the draining standard after being treated. (oil content: 15mg/l, suspended matters: 25mg/l)
- After tank washing, hot work for repair can be carried out ___8___ tank.

> **VOCABULARY ASSISTANT**
>
> physical property 物质性　　guarantee 保障
> concentration 浓度　　　　flammable gas 可燃性气体
> reusable 可重新使用的　　　draining standard 排放标准
> suspended matters 悬浮物

Look at these pictures, can you classify all kinds of tools mentioned in the picture?

A. 2400 tapping machine　　　　B. main stoppling equipment
C. sandwich valve　　　　　　　D. clips of rush to repair
E. stopplers　　　　　　　　　　F. 1200 tapping machine
G. plugging heads　　　　　　　H. 660,760 tapping machines

ENGINEERING MAINTAINING AND REPAIRING UNIT 9

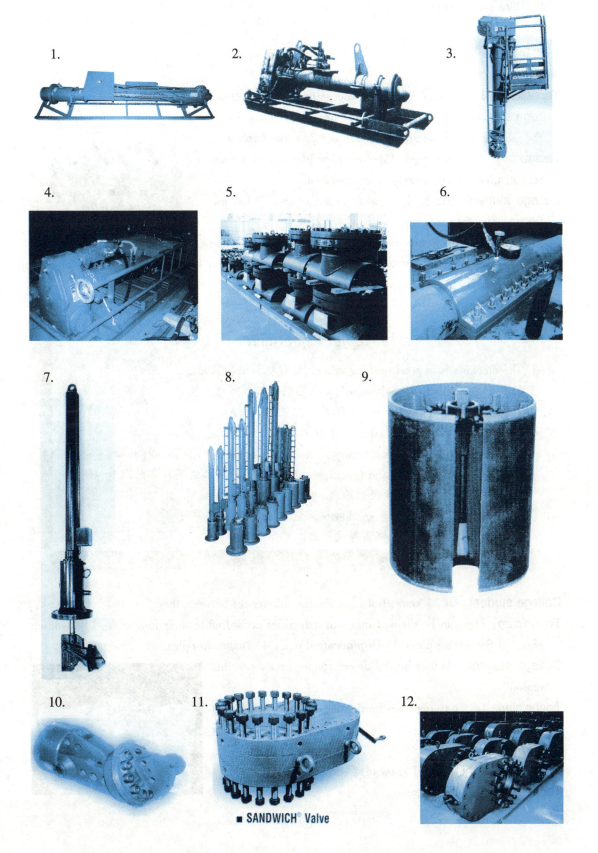

Part Three Dialogues

★ Dialogue One
● Pigs

Technician: Hello, Xiao Wang, are you going to graduate from your college?

College student: Yes, this is the first time that I come here, the job site. Eh, what are they, they are just like **barbell**?

Technician: They are pigs. Pipeline pigs play an important role in pipeline construction and operation.

College student: Pigs? I've never heard of that. What are the purposes for using pigs?

Technician: The main function is 1) to clean out the debris, increase pipeline efficiency and reduce pipeline *corrosion*. 2) to separate dissimilar products. 3) to test pipeline pressure. 4) to inspect corrosion for the wall of pipeline.

> #### Useful Expressions
>
> 1. The machine is in good working order. 这台机器运转良好。
> 2. I felt the machine shakes seriously. 我感到这机器震动严重。
> 3. The machine parts went hot. 这机器零件发热。
> 4. The machine is knocking badly. 这台机器敲击声厉害。
> 5. If there arises any abnormal temperature (unusual noises, vibration), it is necessary to stop the machine and investigate the cause. 如果产生不正常的温升（异常噪音、振动），必须停车查明原因。
> 6. We shall give the machine another trial at 10 o'clock. 我们将在十点钟把这台机器再试一次。

College student: Ok, I know. But what are the differences between them?

Technician: Pigs can be divided into four categories according to their functions: 1) Cleaning pigs; 2) Separating pigs; 3) *Displacement* pigs; 4) *Inspection* pigs.

College student: Do they have different shapes because of this reason?

Technician: Oh, no, pigs can be divided into four categories according to their forms: 1) Disc pigs; 2) Cup pigs; 3) Foam pigs; 4) *Spheres*.

College student: I think I know pigs very well, thanks a lot!

Technician: You are welcome.

ENGINEERING MAINTAINING AND REPAIRING UNIT 9 101

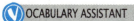OCABULARY ASSISTANT

pig 清管器　　　　barbell 杠铃　　　　corrosion 腐蚀
displacement 置换　inspection 检测　　sphere 橡胶球

Can you translate the following phrases? Try your best!

1. to clean out the debris, increase pipeline efficiency and reduce pipeline corrosion
2. to separate dissimilar products
3. pipeline pressure testing
4. corrosion inspection for the wall of pipeline
5. cleaning pigs　　6. separating pigs　　7. displacement pigs　　8. inspection pigs
9. disc pigs　　　　10. cup pigs　　　　11. foam pigs　　　　　12. spheres

★ **Dialogue Two**
● **Main features and Types**

Worker: Excuse me, may I ask you some questions? What are the main features of hot-tapping, plugging and route *alteration* under pressure and without pipeline *shut-down*?

Engineer: Of course. It has several advantages: advanced process, operation without shut-down, safe and reliable, operation without flame, wide range of usage, without pollution.

Worker: Oh, that's all? That's a wonderful technology. What are the types of *stoppling*?

Engineer: Stoppling can be divided as per whether it is fluid or not: stoppling with shut-down and stoppling without shut-down.

Worker: What about stoppling methods?

Engineer: Physical mechanical stoppling methods can be divided into 4 methods: *suspension* stoppling, *barrel type* stoppling, *folded* stoppling, *bag* stoppling.

Worker: I know. I think I have learned a lot from you. Thank you very much.

OCABULARY ASSISTANT

alteration 改线　　　shut-down 停输　　　stopple 封堵
suspension 悬挂式　　barrel type 桶式　　　folded 折叠式　　bag 囊式

Work with your partner to recite the focus mentioned above.

★ **Dialogue Three**
● **Tank Washing Equipment**

Xiao Li is a visitor. And he comes from a technical college. Mr. Zhang is a specialist.

Xiao Li: Hello, Specialist. What are those, are they tanks?

Mr. Zhang: Yes, you are right. How do you know them, young man?

Xiao Li: I've learned some materials from my book, just the pictures, you know. But I have no chance to see them in my college. Could you tell me in detail?

Mr. Zhang: Of course. Usually, *tank washing* equipment consists of *gas monitoring and oil / water separating system*, two main systems.

Xiao Li: Err, there are many pumps and machines, what are they?

Mr. Zhang: Ha..., two main systems consist of COW unit, gas protection system, gas monitoring system and oil / gas separating system.

Xiao Li: What does COW unit stand for?

Mr. Zhang: That is crude oil washing, it has A, B units: *Filter*, Vacuum pump, Vacuum tank, Recovery pump, *Heat exchanger*, Washing pump, *Air compressor*, Washing machine. Look there!

Xiao Li: I see. What about the other systems?

Mr. Zhang: Gas protection system consists of liquefied nitrogen tank and *liquid nitrogen gasifier*. Gas monitoring system consists of fixed gas *monitor*, portable alarm for harmful gas.

Xiao Li: That must be an oil / water separating device?

Mr. Zhang: You are right. Oil / water separating tank consists of water pump, **biochemical** treatment. Do you know clearly?

Xiao Li: Yes. Thank you very much for your kindness. **Experience is the best teacher**.

Mr. Zhang: That's my pleasure.

VOCABULARY ASSISTANT

tank washing 油罐清洗   filter 过滤器   heat exchanger 换热器
gas monitoring and oil / water separating system 气体检测及油水分离系统
liquid nitrogen 液氮   gasifier 汽化器   monitor 监测器
biochemical 生物化学的   Experience is the best teacher 实践出真知

Read the above dialogue carefully and grasp the main idea according to the VOCABULARY ASSISTANT.

Part Four   Reading

Passage 1

Outline of Tank Mechanical Washing

Generally, the overhaul interval of metal oil storage tanks shall be 5—7 years. Before a thorough inspection and repairs of the storage tank, it is necessary to be thorough cleaned so as to remove all the deposits within tank and meet requirements of repairing hot work.

Manual cleaning method has all kinds of problems such as high labor intensity, long operating period, poor safety factor, low recovery rate of crude oil and environment pollution etc. As a large number of big sized crude oil storage tanks have been constructed and more stresses have been pointed out daily, the manual cleaning is gradually replaced by the mechanical cleaning method.

After oil storage tanks have been put into operation and have reached a certain working cycle, corrosions, deformation, un-even settlement, aging of accessories within tanks, volume affected and changes of stored medium etc. will occur, and thus, partial or

overall maintenance and repair shall be needed so as to ensure safety of the tank and safe operation. And thus, mechanical washing technique will be the best selection for tank refurbishment.

Discuss with your partners.

1. What are the disadvantages of manual cleaning method?
2. Why will mechanical washing technique be the best selection for tank refurbishment?

Passage 2

Principle of Tank Mechanical Washing

The spraying principle is used for mechanical washing. The spray washing equipment, washing tank and the recovery tank are connected with piping and to form a **circulating (cycling) system**. Before washing, nitrogen shall **be injected into** the washing tank to make it a safe working atmosphere with oxygen concentration of less 8% V.

The washer sprays oil which shall be provided by the oil supply tank. The washer sprays oil on the deposits and all surfaces of the **top**, the **shell** and the **bottom plates** in the tank, which can make the deposits **disperse** and dissolve, form a new mixture with the supplied oil. The mixture then shall be transferred into the recovery tank with **the extraction and suction system**. After a certain time of re-cycling deposits, such as **condensed wax** etc., it will be disposed and this is the so-called "crude oil washing" procedure.

VOCABULARY ASSISTANT

circulating (cycling) system 循环系统	be injected into 注入
shell 罐壁	top 罐顶
bottom plate 罐底板	disperse 扩散
the extraction and suction system 抽吸系统	condensed wax 结蜡

Talk about principle of tank mechanical washing in your own words.

Part Five Case Study

Passage 1

Ethylene pipeline rehabilitation project at South Zhuhai Road, Tianyi City: This pipeline transports the ethylene raw material for No.1 Tianyi City Chemical Plant, and the pipeline route should be changed due to the construction of the Zhuhai Road. It should take 10—12 days if traditional pipeline shut-down method was adopted and nearly 9 million *yuan* would be lost. Thanks to the stoppling technique without pipeline shut-down, the work was completed safely with high efficiency not affecting proper pipeline operation and saving a large amount of cost for the owner too.

Passage 2

Pipeline Maintenance & Repair Project for Pengcheng Petroleum Refinery Co.: The pipeline supplies fresh water for the company. It needs to take 6 days if the traditional pipeline shut-down and empty the pipeline method are adopted. Stopping 6 days means a lot to the enterprise with annual profit of 1600 million *yuan*. The stoppling technique without pipeline shut-down makes it possible to repair the pipeline without affecting the proper operation of the line.

> **Discussion:** *In your opinion, how many advantages of stoppling technique without pipeline shut-down are there?*

> **Know about the process principle of typical stoppling techniques without shut-down, translate the following parts, and then give the correct order.**

1—stoppler; 2—*adapter*; 3—special sandwich valve; 4—stoppling *tee*/fitting;
5—pressure balanced *nipple*; 6—pipeline section to be modified; 7—plugging heads;
8—*bypass* tee; 9—bypass sandwich valve; 10—bypass pipe

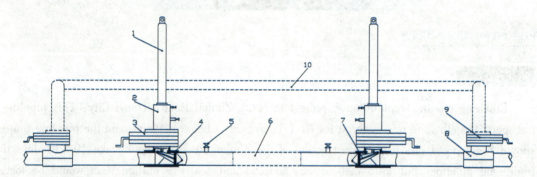

1. pipeline stoppling

2. connect bypass pipe

3. welding the bypass fitting, 2″ pressure balanced nipples and stopple fittings

4. install stoppling fitting and 2″ pressure balanced nipples

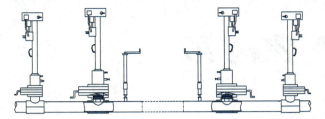

5. installing the blinds onto fitting, fix nuts onto 2″ pressure balanced nipples

6. hot-tapping of 2″ balance, bypass and stoppling hole

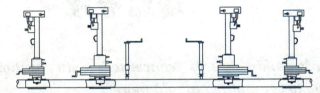

VOCABULARY ASSISTANT

adapter 结合器   tee 三通
nipple 短节   bypass 旁通

Unit 10

Station Management

场站管理

Study the following words and phrases concerned with station management. Learn them by heart and try to add more.

- oil transmission station
- gas transmission station
- maintenance station
- pumping station
- anti-corrosive station
- pipeline metering
- gas quality analysis
- cathodic protection
- dust extraction
- separating
- anti-corrosion
- line patrol
- cathodic protector
- filter
- electric control valve
- pipe(line) cleaning
- pressure booster

Now discuss the following questions with your partner. Please notice that some of the questions are open-ended.

1. How many kinds of stations do you know? What are they for?
2. How many kinds of routine jobs do you know in the daily management of each station?
3. What equipments or facilities are utilized there in these stations?
4. Do you know the processing flow of any station?

Unit 10
Station Management

VOCABULARY ASSISTANT

maintenance 维修
anticorrosive 防腐的
cathodic 阴极的，负极的
booster 调压器
filter 过滤器

AIM

- Learn how to manage different stations concerned with oil and gas

Part One Word Power

Do you know the following stations in the process of oil and gas production? Match them with their Chinese equivalents and try to add more.

oil transmission station	输油站
gas transmission station	防腐站
metering station	输气站
pumping station	泵站、增压站
crude oil treating station	油库
anti-corrosive station	巡线站
tank farm	地下储气库
maintenance station	计量站
underground gas storage	原油处理站

The following are some terms used in the daily management of stations. Can you find the proper Chinese meanings with a dictionary and add more?

gas quality analysis	气质分析
pipeline metering	管道流体计量
cathodic protection	过量增压
overpressurization	阴极保护
pigging and purging	清管和扫线

UNIT 10 STATION MANAGEMENT

Here are some facilities and equipments. Do you know what they are in Chinese? And can you list some others?

1. pressure booster
2. cathodic protector
3. floating roofed tank
4. degassing column
5. oil and gas separator
6. electric control valve
7. heating furnace
8. separator
9. filter
10. compressor

A. 脱气塔
B. 增压器
C. 阴极保护器
D. 浮顶罐
E. 加热炉
F. 油气分离器
G. 电动阀
H. 压缩机
I. 分离器
J. 过滤器

Do you know more about station management? Try to make up as many dialogues as possible with what you've already known.

Part Two   Listening

Listen to the passages about security knowledge of tank farm and pumping station. Fill in the blanks with the proper words.

Passage 1

Petroleum and its products are flammable, _____1_____, and evaporable, so petroleum products can be classified to different _____2_____ classes according to their flash point. _____3_____ point is often the control criterion of security. When petroleum and its _____4_____ are transported and stored, proper flameproof _____5_____ must be adopted in order to prevent fire. _____6_____ must be forbidden in tank farm and pumping station.

Do not wear shoes with _____7_____ hobnail or heel plate.
Do not wear clothes that is easy to produce static _____8_____.
Oil leaking should be _____9_____ in tank farm and pumping station.
Facilities of oil transporting and storing should adopt grounding in tank farm and pumping station.
Do not knock on tank or pipeline with metallic _____10_____.

VOCABULARY ASSISTANT

flammable 易燃的,可燃性的   evaporable 易蒸发性的,蒸发性的
hobnail 平头钉   static 静态的,静力的
grounding 接地   metallic 金属(性)的

Listen again and answer the following questions.

1. What should we do to prevent fire in petroleum transportation?
2. What must be forbidden in tank farm and pumping station?
3. What kind of shoes and clothes should one wear in a tank farm?

Passage 2

The other danger in oil transporting and storing is the fire and explosion caused by static electricity. When_____1_____ petroleum and its products, the fraction among oil molecules, _____2_____, wall of containers will produce static electricity. Because petroleum and its products are_____3_____, the static electricity will get together. When_____4_____adds to a certain level, the static electricity discharge will occur and it will lead to a fire or_____5_____, especially when oil pass non-metallic pipeline or filtration net made up of_____6_____or felt in pipeline, the voltage of static electricity will be much higher and more dangerous.

In order to prevent the fire_____7_____caused by static electricity, all_____8_____and pipelines must have nice _____9_____devices. In order to insure the grounding resistance less than 10 ohm,_____10_____must be often done.

VOCABULARY ASSISTANT

molecule 分子,小粒   filtration 过滤,筛选
felt 毡,毡制品   ohm 欧姆(电阻单位)

Listen again and answer the following questions.

1. What can cause fire and explosion in oil transporting and storing?
2. How does static electricity happen?
3. How to prevent fire caused by static electricity?

Passage 3

Petroleum and its products have toxicity to a certain extent, especially its ____1____. The vapor of the petroleum will pass the skin, respiratory system and digestive ____2____ and go into the human body.

At the workaround of ____3____ farm and pumping station, the concentration of oil vapor must be strictly ____4____. When the concentration of oil vapor reaches 5—10 mg/l, workers there will get a ____5____; when it reaches 30—40 mg/l, they will be ____6____ in 5—10 minutes. So if the worker has to work in a condition with ____7____ concentration of oil vapor, he must wear ____8____ and special ____9____ to prevent ____10____.

Listen again and answer the following questions.

1. How will the vapor of petroleum do harm to our health?
2. What must be strictly controlled at a tank farm?
3. What's the probable reason for one's headache in a tank farm?
4. What can cause death?
5. How can we prevent ourselves from the vapor of petroleum?

VOCABULARY ASSISTANT

toxicity 毒性 respiratory 呼吸的
digestive system 消化系统 workaround 工作区

Part Three Dialogues

Read and act out the dialogues with your partner.

Two students, Winnie and Bob, are talking about a gas transmission station.

★ Dialogue One

W: Hello, Bob! Can you tell me something about the gas transmission station?

B: Of course! What do you want to know?

W: Well, I wonder what equipments and facilities are in the gas transmission station.

B: Um... First, there are separators, gas filters, and **dust catchers**.

W: I know that the separator is used to remove the liquids and some other impurities from the gas. But what is a filter for?

B: The filter is used to remove the smaller solid impurities that are still left after the separation, such as **rust** and **iron scraps** in the pipeline. It has the similar function to a dust catcher, which removes mainly the dust in the gas.

W: I see. So the three are all used to improve the quality of the natural gas?

B: Yes. You're right.

★ Dialogue Two

W: Anything else?

B: Yes. There is also the **spherical pig trap** used to launch and receive pigs for pigging the pipeline.

W: Pigging the pipeline?

B: Yes. Pigging here means to clear the **filth** from the pipeline.

W: (*Nodding*) Oh, I see. And any other equipments?

B: Yeah! There are heaters generally equipped in the northern part of China where it is very cold to heat the natural gas.

W: Heat the gas?

B: Yes. We heat the gas and raise its temperature with the purpose to prevent the formation of hydrates.

W: Oh, yes. I know hydrates will result in a total or partial blockage of the pipeline, right?

B: That's it!

★ **Dialogue Three**

B: And there are ***self-act pressure regulators*** used to regulate the gas pressure of the station.
W: Uh-huh.
B: ***Valves*** to control the pressure and flow of the gas.
W: Yes.
B: And ***safety valves*** to make sure that all the pipeline equipments work in the range of pressures allowable.
W: So, all these make everything and everybody free from danger?
B: Yes. And there are also different types of gauges or meters which are serving the same purpose.
W: Like ***flow meter***, ***thermometer***, and ***pressure gauge***?
B: Yeah! Safety first!

> **VOCABULARY ASSISTANT**
>
> dust catcher 除尘器　　rust 铁锈　　iron scrap 铁屑
> spherical pig trap 清管球收发筒　　filth 污物
> self-act pressure regulator 自力式压力调节器
> valve 阀门　　safety valve 安全阀　　flow meter 流量计
> thermometer 温度计　　pressure gauge 压力表

Act out the dialogues in pairs and then discuss the following questions.

1. How many kinds of equipments and facilities do you know in a gas transmission?
2. What does a separator do?
3. Do you know the functions of gas filters and dust catchers?
4. What heaters are used for? Why?
5. Are there any equipments or facilities for safety? What are they?

Read through the following remarks and instructions used in the daily management of a gas station. Learn them by heart and then make up dialogues with some of them.

About Valves

> Open/Close the plug valve. 打开/关闭旋塞阀。
> Open/Close the electric ball valve. 打开/关闭电动球阀。
> Open/Close the manual ball valve. 打开/关闭手动球阀。
> Open/Close the gate valve. 打开/关闭闸板阀。
> Open/Close the vent valve. 打开/关闭放空阀。
> Open/Close the throttle and cut-off vent valve. 打开/关闭节流截止放空阀。

Open/Close the regulating valve. 打开/关闭调压阀。
Open/Close the active pressurizing valve. 打开/关闭主动密封阀。
Open/Close the gas shutoff valve(GOV). 打开/关闭气液联动阀。
Open/Close the suction valve. 打开/关闭吸气阀。
Open/Close the discharge valve. 打开/关闭排气阀。
Open/Close the station-bypass valve. 打开/关闭旁通阀。
Open/Close the quick blind flange. 打开/关闭快开盲板。
Open/Close the drain valve. 打开/关闭排污阀。
Open/Close the balance valve. 打开/关闭平衡阀。

About Generators

Add oil/antifreeze to generator. 给发电机加油/防冻液。
Replace the lube of generator. 给发电机换润滑油。
Replace generator's lube filter element. 给发电机换机油滤芯。
Replace generator's diesel oil filter element. 给发电机换柴油滤芯。
Replace generator's air filter element. 给发电机换空气滤芯。
Disconnect the power of generator. 断开发电机的供电开关。
How much is the oil pressure of generator? 发电机的油压是多少?
How much is the water temperature of generator? 发电机的水温是多少?
How much is the output pressure of generator? 发电机的输出电压是多少?
How much is the output power of generator? 发电机的输出功率是多少?
How much is the output current of generator? 发电机的输出电流是多少?

About Cathodic Protection

Check the state of the cathodic protection machine.
检查阴保机的工作状态。
Report the working voltage of the cathodic protection machine.
报告阴保机的工作电压。
Report the working current of the cathodic protection machine.
报告阴保机的工作电流。
How much is the working voltage of the cathodic protection machine?
阴保机的工作电压是多少?
How much is the working current of the cathodic protection machine?
阴保机的工作电流是多少?
The cathodic protection of this pipeline is very well.
管线阴极保护很好。
The cathodic current is 0.5 mA. 阴极保护电流是 0.5 mA。
Test the electric potential and record it. 检查电压并做记录。

About Fire

Is everything all right here? 你们这里的情况正常吗？
I smelled the peculiar smell in the machine room. 我在机房闻到了异味。
Open the ventilator in the generator room. 打开发电机房的换气扇。
Electric spark can ignite natural gas. 电火花可使天然气着火。
Natural gas is flammable and explosive. 天然气是易燃、易爆的物品。
Check fire protection system. 检查消防系统。
Please turn off the light. 请随手关灯。
It is necessary to forbid kindling for preventing blast.
禁绝火种是防止气体爆炸的必备条件。
The maneuver of fire fighting will be made tomorrow.
明天将进行消防演习。

About Safety Operation

Don't operate the equipments without command. 进入场站请听从指挥，不准操作设备。
Check leak points of devices in the site. 场站设备检漏。
The pressure transducer is out of order, check it please. 压力传感器显示故障，请检查。
Check the device of the blow-down site. 检查放空点装置。
Check the blow-down area. 检查放空区。
Check the working state of the generator set.
检查发电机组的工作状态。
Check the switch state of the distribution ark.
检查配电柜的开关状态。
I find there is a leak in the valve.
我发现阀门有内漏现象。
The remote function of the valve does not work.
这个阀门的远控功能失灵了。

Read through the following remarks about a gas storage (储气库). *Try to translate them into Chinese and then make up dialogues with some of them in groups.*

1. This underground gas storage is the extend-project of the underground gas storage project, which is an accessorial project of Shaanjing pipelines.
2. The purpose is to guarantee that the natural gas transmitted safely and stably to Beijing, to solve the problem of seasonal peak and emergency gas supply in special instance.
3. The working-range of design pressure of the gas storage is 13Mpa to 25Mpa, the maximal volume of the gas storage is 4.65×108 m^3, including base gas tolerance 1.5×108 m^3, underlay gas tolerance 0.95×108 m^3, and effective working-gas tolerance 2.17×108 m^3.
4. The ground was broken for this project on September 20th, 2001, and was completed on June 10th, 2002. The project consists of 5 new gas injection-production wells, 2 reused gas wells and processing station with daily injection capability of 0.5—1 million cubic meters, supply capability of 2 million cubic meters.
5. The capacity of gas process devices is about 2 million cubic meters every day.
6. Normally, the dew-point of processed-gas is -5℃.
7. gas well → throttle valve → gas process devices (separate, measure, and dew point control) → outlet to Beijing.
8. The technology of injecting carbinol to the port of the gas well, the technology of injecting glycol to the dew point process devices, and the technology of glycol regeneration are adopted in the craftwork of gas process.
9. The compressor suction pressure was designed from 1.8 to 2.5MPa (G), and the discharge pressure was from 18 to 27MPa (G).
10. The injection capacity of the two compressors is 100×104s m^3/d (Condition of: 2.1MPa (G) suction pressure, 24MPa (G) discharge pressure).
11. The compressor group is adopted with PLC unit control panel, which can start, control and stop the compressor, by local and remote control.
12. The craftwork of inject gas is: Gas from Shaanjing pipeline → separator → filter → compressor → gas well.

Part Four Reading

Passage 1

Environment Protection in Station Management

In order to ensure a smooth, safe oil or gas transportation and distribution, and to maintain a neat pleasant environment, a scientific management is necessary to all the stations concerned. So we need to improve constantly the management system and perfect all the regulations, in addition to improving the technical work.

The following are a few regulations concerned with ecological or environmental protection that must be obeyed in nearly all stations.

☆ The pollution control measures must be taken for waste gas, water, solid, noise, **vibration**, **radioactivity**, **electromagnetic radiation**, **foul odor**, **pathogen**, garbage that are generated in production or life but **toxic** and harmful. After the treatment or disposal of them, **in compliance with** the state or local discharge criteria, they could be discharged in order to protect the environment from being damaged and polluted.

☆ In order to control atmosphere pollution, melting of bitumen and burning of oils, **asphalt felt**, rubber, plastics and some other chemical raw materials that may generate toxic and harmful smoke and foul odor must be strictly controlled in **populous** areas.

☆ Discharge beyond standard of oils, acid liquor, **alkali** liquor, mud fluid and highly toxic materials such as **mercury**, **arsenic**, **chromium**, lead, **cyanide** as well as radioactive solid wastes into waters shall be forbidden in order to control water pollution. Discharge or dump of industrial waste **slag**, production or **sanitary garbage** into waters shall also be forbidden. No pileup of toxic and harmful waste solids and sanitary garbage shall be allowed.

☆ All the pump stations for gathering or transmission pipelines should enhance equipment management; leakage and drips should be got rid of; the **leak rate of the gasket-type seal point** should be no more than two **millesimal**.

VOCABULARY ASSISTANT

vibration 振动
radioactivity 放射性
electromagnetic radiation 电磁波幅射
foul odor 恶臭
pathogen 微生物,病原体
asphalt felt 油毛毡
populous 人口多的,人口稠密的
alkali 碱性的
mercury 水银,汞

arsenic 砷, 砒霜
chromium 铬
cyanide 氰化物
slag 矿渣,炉渣
toxic 有毒的
in compliance with 遵照……行事
sanitary garbage 生活垃圾
leak rate of the gasket-type seal point 静密封点泄漏率
millesimal 千分之一

Discuss the following questions after reading.

1. What do you think is the most important in station management?
2. What should we do to prevent pollution and protect the environment?
3. How many kinds of garbage do you know? What are they?
4. What kinds of wastes are toxic and harmful?

Passage 2

Tank Cleaning

Crude oil storage tanks, whether vaulted tanks or floating roofed tanks, need to be inspected, repaired and removed the deposits periodically. For the time being, most of storage tanks in China are cleaned manually, but that may cause many problems such as high intensity of labor, long period of operation, poor safety, low recovery and environmental pollution, etc. As a large number of big sized crude oil storage tanks have been constructed, and more attention has been paid nowadays to the environment, manual tank cleaning cannot meet the requirements of development and environment protection any longer.

Mechanical washing technique is one of the major techniques for onshore crude oil storage tanks. This method has effectively raised the mechanical washing level and made true of the mechanical washing for large sized storage tanks, and thus changed the situation of mere manual cleaning.

Super-large metal storage tanks of 150,000 m^3 are under designing in China now. 3—5 years after the tanks' being put into operation, problems such as corrosion, deformation, uneven settlement, **aging of heating coils**, **impeded drainage** will occur, and the owner has to consider the partial or overall maintenance and repair for the sake of safety. Therefore, mechanical washing of the tank will provide suitable condition for the **refurbishment**. In addition, the medium stored in a tank may be changed, for example, from crude oil to product oil, etc., and thorough cleaning is also required to avoid the mutual pollution.

The cost of mechanical tank washing will be 50—60% more than that of manual cleaning owing to the cost increase for transportation, installation and safe protection of COM (crude oil storage tank mechanical washing) system. However, manual tank cleaning will waste the bottom oil as the long time deposited oil has high wax content, more contamination, poor physical property and flow ability, all of which will bring about hidden **perils** for transportation if effective treatment has not been conducted. Besides, the oil receiving company will feel difficult to suit with such a sudden change.

During mechanical washing process, the tank bottom will be treated repeatedly and can achieve normal oil physical property, so the oil may be transferred into other tanks or be transported to down-stream users directly. In this way, less loss of tank bottom oil is achieved, and the owner may enjoy less expense in total economic benefit.

VOCABULARY ASSISTANT

aging of heating coils 罐内加热盘管老化　　impeded drainage 排水管线不畅
refurbishment 整修　　peril 隐患

Discuss the following questions after reading.

1. What are the two methods of crude oil storage tank cleaning?
2. What is the advantage of mechanical cleaning?
3. Does manual cleaning have any advantage over mechanical cleaning?
4. If you are an owner of some large storage tanks, which method are you likely to choose to clean your tanks? Why?

KEY TO QUESTIONS

Unit 1
Pipeline Exploration and Designing

Part One　Word Power

　　1—J　2—F　3—H　4—I　5—A　6—G　7—B　8—D　9—E　10—C

Part Two　Listening

1. remarkable　2. efficiency　3. energy　4. concludes　5. consume　6. products　7. compared　8. consumption　9. precisely　10. crude

Part Four　Reading

　　1. 其中许多管道的输送能力和输油品种的灵活性都很大。

　　2. 在其他国家，使用成品油管道把海岸边炼油厂的或油港卸下的成品油送到内陆人口稠密的地区。

　　3. 在同一条管道内输送一种以上的油品，显然比输送单一品种油品需要更完善的监控措施。

Unit 2
Pipeline Engineering

Part One　Word Power

　　1—E　2—F　3—I　4—H　5—D　6—A　7—J　8—G　9—B　10—C

1. ditching, crossing　2. Backfilling the trench　3. cleaning up　4. testing　5. bending
6. pipe cleaning, coating and wrapping　7. Lowering-in　8. welding　9. backfilling

Part Two　Listening

1. handling　2. combined　3. phase　4. success　5. equipment　6. quantities　7. selected　8. efficient　9. joints　10. route

Part Four　Reading

　　1. T　2. F　3. F　4. T　5. T　6. F

Unit 3
Equipment Installation

Part One   Word Power

A—6 B—7 C—9 D—14 E—1 F—18 G—10 H—4 I—12 J—20 K—15 L—19 M—3 N—17 O—5 P—2 Q—11 R—8 S—13 T—16

Part Two   Listening

1. structures 2. Olympic 3. construction 4. equipment 5. crucial 6. hoisting 7. underwent 8. supportive 9. staff 10. overcame

Part Three   Dialogues

Do the following exercises by translating the Chinese into English.

1. When will the installation of this equipment be completed?
2. Engineer Wang is in charge of the installation work today.
3. Check over the tools and make sure whether all of them are in good condition.
4. I'll level it at once, then pave the steel plates.
5. I felt the machine shakes seriously.

Use the correct form of the words from the box to complete the sentences.

a. erection b. instruction c. out of order d. machinery e. switch f. adjusted g. compelled h. operate i. reliable j. abnormal

The following is the valve installation sequence, could you put them in correct order? Then match the sentences (a-g) with each step.

1—checking 2—prefabricating 3—lifting in place 4—entirety pressure test 5—anticorrosion 6—clearance

a—2 b—4 c—1 d—3 e—6 f—7 g—5

Unit 4
Anticorrosion Pipeline

Part One   Word Power

A—3 B—4 C—8 D—5 E—9 F—11 G—19 H—2 I—12 J—1 K—10 L—7 M—6 N—16 O—18 P—13 Q—14 R—20 S—15 T—17

Part Two   Listening

1. occur 2. gathers 3. depends 4. conditions 5. removal 6. monitoring 7. reportable 8. percentage 9. delivery 10. simplify

Part Three Dialogues

Do the following exercises by translating the Chinese into English.

1. What is the function of the coal-tar in preventing corrosion?
2. The metal parts can be protected from corrosion by painting.
3. The anticorrosion materials shall be stored in a dry place to prevent from damp and sunshine directly irradiating.
4. If the pipeline fittings become rusty, rust will have to be cleaned.
5. The rust results from oxygen acting on metals.

Use the correct form of the words from the box to complete the sentences.

a. cleaned b. foreign c. coated d. exterior e. covering f. damp g. rust h. corroded i. protected j. according to

The following is the anticorrosion sequence in Plants, could you put them in correct order? Then match the sentences (a-i) with each step.

1. preparation → 2. portage and placement → 3. cleaning surface → 4. blast cleaning → 5. removing dust → 6. spraying paint → 7. coating solidifying → 8. checking and acceptance → 9. taking construction records

a. 8 b. 3 c. 5 d. 1 e. 4 f. 7 g. 6 h. 2 i. 9

Unit 5

Oil and Gas Transportation

Part One Word Power

C—1; I—2; D—3; A—4; F—5; B—6; E—7; G—8; J—9; H—10

Part Two Listening

Passage 1

1. crude; 2. gas; 3. impurities; 4. mixture; 5. homogeneous; 6. emulsion; 7. sediment; 8. removed; 9. separation; 10. treatment

Passage 2

1. shipment; 2. lease; 3. volumes; 4. pipeline; 5. measured; 6. manually; 7. calculated; 8. storage; 9. gathering; 10. volumes

Passage 3

1. gas-gathering; 2. transmission; 3. crude; 4. equipments; 5. pressures; 6. compressors; 7. pumps; 8. direct

Unit 6

Welding Engineering

Part One   Word Power

Part A

1—F 2—K 3—H 4—B 5—L 6—J 7—D 8—A 9—C 10—G 11—E 12—I

Part B

1—D 2—N 3—R 4—J 5—M 6—K 7—Q 8—O 9—S 10—A 11—E 12—T
13—C 14—G 15—F 16—L 17—H 18—B 9—I 20—P

Part Two   Listening

Passage 1

1. arc   2. particular   3. development   4. current   5. means   6. application   7. electrodes

8. device   9. flow   10. medium

Passage 2

1. Welding   2. sections   3. fabrication   4. applications   5. shielded   6. metal   7. mechanized

8. manual   9. mainline   10. requirements

Part Three   Dialogues

The following is the process showing how air filters should be serviced regularly. First please match them, and then put them into correct order.

1—c—D 2—e—B 3—a—F 4—f—E 5—h—H 6—b—C 7—j—J 8—i—I 9—d—B
10—g—A

Discuss with your partners and translate the following sentences.

1. 整个焊接过程包括：引弧、焊接、熄弧。
2. Safety shall be paid attention to when using welding liquid gas bottle.
3. 焊接烟尘中有大量有害气体。
4. Electrode shall be kept in the dryer to prevent the covering from being damped.
5. 焊条分为药皮和焊芯。
6. Please open the acetylene bottle.
7. 焊接电源分为交流焊机和直流焊机两种。
8. Is cover glass available?
9. 电源极性应符合工艺要求。
10. DC welding machine may adopt straight polarity or reversed polarity.

KEY TO QUESTIONS

Use the correct form of the words from the box to complete the sentences and translate them.

1. weldablity 碳当量是衡量材料焊接性好坏的重要指标。
2. positive 正接是工件接电源正极。
3. voltage 焊机的空载电压是多少？
4. Acid 酸性焊条对铁锈不敏感。
5. workshop 焊接车间通风要好。
6. requirement 焊接用材应符合要求。

Unit 7
Engineering Monitoring

Part One Word Power

Part A

1—I 2—G 3—L 4—J 5—D 6—K 7—A 8—E 9—B 10—H 11—C 12—F

Part B

1—B 2—L 3—H 4—K 5—N 6—A 7—D 8—I 9—E 10—R 11—Q 12—O 13—T 14—S 15—M 16—P 17—C 18—F 19—J 20—G

Discuss with your partners and translate the following sentences.

1. Do you have any reference materials about this project?
2. 这事交给我们去办吧。
3. Put on your safety helmet, please.
4. 当心！快躲开！
5. Something's wrong with the machine.
6. 停机,断电。
7. What's wrong with the engine?
8. 我们已按照进度完成了这道工序。
9. Do you know how to adjust this new machine?
10. 这台设备是由卖方提供的。

Use the correct form of the words from the box to complete the sentences and translate them.

1. completed 这是整体设备,那是现场制作设备。
2. characteristic 你能告诉我们有关这个工程的技术特性吗？
3. satisfied 试运行的结果我们感到满意。
4. risky 我们要防止违章冒险作业。
5. avert 我们应该制定操作规则防止事故发生。
6. disassemble 他们已经学会了如何安全地拆卸和安装这些机器了。
7. measures 应该采取严格的安全措施以便工程能顺利地完成。
8. inspection 我们计划在星期二以前完成设备检查工作。

Part Two Listening

Passage 1

1. ditch 2. option 3. level 4. contractor 5. right-of-way 6. practical 7. install
8. equipment 9. Vehicles 10. temporary

Passage 2

1. projects 2. construction 3. worksites 4. reports 5. materials 6. generally
7. requirements 8. regular 9. occurs 10. complete

Passage 3

1. responsibilities 2. supervisor 3. environment 4. implementation 5. examine
6. relevant 7. personnel 8. conduct 9. suggestions 10. instruction

Part Four Reading

Please identify the following statements are true or false.

1—F 2—T 3—T 4—F 5—T

Unit 8
HSE

Part One Word Power

1—F 2—B 3—G 4—A 5—I 6—C 7—T 8—H 9—M 10—D 11—R 12—J
13—E 14—P 15—N 16—O 17—S 18—Q 19—L 20—K

Part Two Listening

Listen to the following passage about mental health carefully and try to fill in the blanks.

1. tension 2. straight 3. perspective 4. releases 5. physical

Listen to the following dialogue about check-up carefully (3 times) and try to fill in the blanks.

1. Why 2. would 3. get 4. had 5. think 6. go to see 7. serious illnesses 8. at least
9. own good 10. deep breath 11. leading 12. lung cancer 13. quit 14. kick 15. classes

Listen to the dialogue between Human Resources Manager (HR) and Company President (CP) and then fill in the blanks.

1. health and safety 2. draft 3. insurance 4. company-wide 5. premises 6. fault 7. fire-aid
8. emergency 9. trained 10. volunteers

Part Three Dialogues

Use the correct form of the words from the box to complete the sentences and translate them.

1. updated 应急部署表需要更新。
2. belt 高空作业要系好保险带。
3. engine 应急发电机应有两套独立的启动方法。
4. switchboard 清洁应急配电盘内部。
5. insulated 我们的电动工具都是双重绝缘的并符合国际安全标准。
6. procedure 在任何时间都应遵守安全程序。

Part Five Case Study

1. Delta 2. four 3. network 4. artificial 5. sensitive 6. budget 7. Ceiling-crossing 8. measures 9. awarded

Unit 9
Engineering Maintaining and Repairing

Part One Word Power

1—F 2—D 3—H 4—E 5—A 6—C 7—O 8—I 9—B 10—G 11—P 12—Q 13—J 14—N 15—K 16—T 17—L 18—S 19—R 20—M

Part Two Listening

Listen to the following passage about HOT-TAPPING AND PLUGGING three times and try to fill in the blanks. Grasp the main idea of the two items.

1. plugging 2. maintenance 3. emergency 4. the rush to 5. pipe 6. off-take 7. shutdown 8. adopted 9. hot-tapping and plugging 10. interference

Listen to the following passage about process of tank mechanical washing three times and try to fill in the blanks. Grasp the main idea of the two items.

1. mechanical 2. recovery 3. connecting 4. sprays 5. flow 6. condensates 7. crude 8. component 9. filtered 10. circulation

Use the correct form of the words from the box to complete the passage and translate it.

1. recovery 2. affect 3. cleaned 4. seen 5. without 6. hidden 7. pollution 8. within

Translation: Features of mechanical washing technique

机械清洗技术特点

- 原油回收率高,回收率达 98%以上。
- 应用蒸汽间接加热,不影响原油的物性。
- 可以清洗人工方式无法处理的高淤积(2 米以上)油罐。
- 机械清洗工艺使用原油作为清洗介质,在一定温度、压力和流量条件下,被清洗表面均露出金属本底。
- 清罐周期短。机械清洗工艺方法,它不受天气及环境的影响,因此效率高、施工期有保证。
- 安全有保障。使用氮气控制罐内氧气和可燃性气体浓度,避免了因清洗机射流过程中产生静电可能带来的不安全隐患。
- 清洗环境良好,不污染环境。经油水分离工艺,充分回收可再利用油品,最终清洗用水经处理后,达到排放标准。(含油量:15 mg/l,悬浮物含量:25 mg/l)
- 清洗结束后,可在罐内进行维修动火作业。

Look at these pictures, can you classify all kinds of tools mentioned in the picture?

A—1 B—4,5 C—11,12 D—6 E—7,8 F—2 G—9,10 H—3

Part Three   Dialogues

Can you translate the following phrases? Try your best!

1. 清扫管道内的碎片,增加管线效率,减少腐蚀
2. 隔离不同介质
3. 管线打压试验
4. 管线管壁腐蚀测试
5. 扫线用清管器
6. 隔离用清管器
7. 置换用清管器
8. 检测用清管器
9. 直型清管器
10. 碟形清管器
11. 泡沫清管器
12. 橡胶球型清管器

Part Five   Case Study

Know about the process principle of typical stoppling techniques without shut-down, translate the following parts, and then give the correct order.

3—Process A 6—Process B 2—Process C 1—Process D 4—Process E 5—Process F

1—封堵器 2—封堵结合器 3—封堵夹板阀 4—封堵三通 5—压力平衡短节 6—维修改造管段 7—封堵头 8—旁通三通 9—旁通夹板阀 10—旁通管道

A. 焊接旁通三通、2"压力平衡短节及封堵三通

B. 连接旁通管线

C. 开 2"孔、旁通孔和封堵孔

D. 管线封堵

E. 三通安装塞堵、2"压力平衡孔安装丝堵

F. 三通安装盲板,2"压力平衡短节安装螺帽

Unit 10
Station Management

Part One　Word Power

1—B；2—C；3—D；4—A；5—F；6—G；7—E；8—I；9—J；10—H

Part Two　Listening

Passage 1

1. explosive；2. danger；3. Flash；4. products；5. regulations；6. Smoking；7. iron；8. electricity；9. forbidden；10. tools

Passage 2

1. transporting；2. pipelines；3. non-conductors；4. voltage；5. explosion；6. silk；7. accident；8. containers；9. grounding；10. inspection

Passage 3

1. vapor；2. system；3. tank；4. controlled；5. headache；6. dead；7. high；8. mask；9. clothes；10. poisoning

Part Three　Dialogues

1. 该地下储气库是陕京输气管道的配套工程——地下储气库的二期工程。
2. 其建设目的是为了保证向北京平稳供气，实现用气调峰以及特殊情况下的紧急供气。
3. 气库设计运行压力区间为 13—25 MPa，最大库容量 $4.65×10^8$ m³，其中基础垫气量为 $1.50×10^8$ m³，附加垫气量 $0.95×10^8$ m³，有效工作气量 $2.17×10^8$ m³。
4. 2001 年 9 月 20 日投入储气库建设，2002 年 6 月 10 日建设完成，渐成规模：注采井 5 口、采气井 2 口，采气能力 200 万方/日；日注气 $50-100×10^4$ m³。
5. 天然气处理装置日处理量每天两百万。
6. 正常情况下，出站天然气水烃露点低于-5℃。
7. 注采井 → 节流阀 → 气体处理装置（分离、计量、露点控制）→ 北京
8. 在处理工艺中采用了井口注甲醇、露点控制注乙二醇以及乙二醇回收重复利用工艺。
9. 天然气进口压力为 1.8-2.5 MPa(G)，出口压力为 18.0-27.0 MPa(G)
10. 在进口压力为 2.1 MPa(G)，出口压力为 24 MPa(G)设计条件下，两台压缩机组的排量为 $100×10^4$s m³/d。
11. 压缩机组采用 PLC 单机控制盘，可实现就地/远程启机、加载、排量控制及卸载、停机全自动操作。
12. 其注气工艺为：陕京来气 → 分离器 → 过滤器 → 压缩机 → 注采井。

Vocabulary

absorption *n.* 吸收	Unit 5	barbell *n.* 杠铃	Unit 9
access *n.* 进入	Unit 7	barge *n.* 驳船	Unit 1
acetylene *n.* 乙炔	Unit 6	batched *n.* 混油	Unit 1
adapter *n.* 结合器	Unit 9	benzene *n.* 苯	Unit 5
additional *adj.* 额外的	Unit 7	berm *n.* 护道,傍山道	Unit 3
adequate *adj.* 足够的	Unit 8	bevel *n.* 坡口	Unit 3
adjacent *adj.* 附近的	Unit 7	bid *n.* 投标	Unit 7
adjust *v.* 调整	Unit 7	biochemical *adj.* 生物化学的	Unit 9
adsorption *n.* 吸附	Unit 5	bitumen *n.* 沥青	Unit 4
affect *v.* 影响	Unit 6	blast *v./n.* 炸开	Unit 7
affinity *n.* 吸引力	Unit 5	blasting *n.* 爆破	Unit 3
alkali *adj.* 碱性的	Unit 10	blueprint *n.* 蓝图,详细的计划	Unit 7
allocation *n.* 分配	Unit 8	bolster *n.* 垫子	Unit 3
alteration *n.* 改线	Unit 9	booster *n.* 调压器	Unit 10
alternated *adj.* 交流的,交替的	Unit 6	bracket *n.* 托架,支架	Unit 4
ambulance *n.* 救护车	Unit 8	brittleness *n.* 脆	Unit 6
annular *adj.* 环形的	Unit 4	bunk *n.* 铺位	Unit 3
antibiotics *n.* 抗生素	Unit 8	bypass *n.* 旁通	Unit 9
anticorrosion *n.* 防腐	Unit 1	canvas *n.* 帆布	Unit 3
anti-corrosive *adj.* 防腐的	Unit 10	capacity *n.* 能力,容量	Unit 1
apparatus *n.* 设备	Unit 1	cathodic *adj.* 阴极的,负极的	Unit 10
application *n.* 应用	Unit 6	characteristic *n.* 特点,特性	Unit 6
arbitration *n.* 仲裁,裁定	Unit 8	chisel *n.* 凿子	Unit 9
arc *n.* 弧,弓形	Unit 3	chock *v./n.* 用楔子垫	Unit 3
arid *adj.* 干燥的	Unit 8	chromium *n.* 铬	Unit 10
arrange *v.* 安排	Unit 7	circumference *n.* 圆周	Unit 3
arsenic *n.* 砷,砒霜	Unit 10	clamp *n.* 夹钳	Unit 7
article *n.* 物品	Unit 4	classify *v.* 分类	Unit 6
assemble *v.* 安装	Unit 3	cleaning *n.* 洗油,去油,清洗	Unit 9
assessment *n.* 估价,评价额	Unit 8	clevis *n.* U形夹,马蹄铁	Unit 3
assign *v.* 指派	Unit 7	CM 建筑工程管理	Unit 7
attach *v.* 附加	Unit 8	coalescence 合并	Unit 5
available *adj.* 可利用的	Unit 3	coaltar *n.* 煤焦油	Unit 2
backfilling *n.* 回填	Unit 2	coefficient *n.* 系数	Unit 3
backhoe *n.* (有伸缩挖掘装置的)锄耕机	Unit 2	collocation *n.* 排列,配置	Unit 3
bag *n.* 囊式	Unit 9	commitment *n.* 责任;承担义务	Unit 5

component *n.* 部件	Unit 6	detergent *n.* 清洁剂	Unit 4
compressor *n.* 压缩机	Unit 1	detour *n./v.* 便道,迂路	Unit 8
comprise *v.* 包含	Unit 1	deviation *n.* 偏差	Unit 1
conceive *v.* 构思	Unit 6	diameter *n.* 直径	Unit 5
concentration *n.* 浓度	Unit 9	diarrhea *n.* 腹泻	Unit 8
concrete *n.* 混凝土	Unit 3	diesel *n.* 柴油	Unit 1
condensate *n.* 凝结物	Unit 9	discard *v.* 丢弃,抛弃	Unit 3
condense *vi.* 浓缩,凝结	Unit 5	discharge *v./n.* 放电	Unit 6
conductivity *n.* 传导性	Unit 6	discipline *n.* 纪律	Unit 8
considerable *adj.* 大量的	Unit 7	dispensary *n.* 医护室	Unit 8
consistency *n.* 言行一致	Unit 8	disperse *v.* 扩散	Unit 9
consolidate *v.* 巩固	Unit 8	displacement *n.* 置换	Unit 9
constitute *v.* 构成	Unit 6	dispose *v.* 处理	Unit 7
consume *v.* 消耗	Unit 1	dissolve *v.* 溶解	Unit 6
contactor *n.* 混合器,萃取器	Unit 5	distribution *n.* 分发,分配管网	Unit 1
container *n.* 货柜	Unit 3	ditching *n.* 挖沟	Unit 2
contaminant *n.* 污染物	Unit 4	drainage *n.* 排水	Unit 7
contract *n.* 合同	Unit 7	dryer *n.* 干燥箱	Unit 6
contractor *n.* 承包商	Unit 7	elaboration *n.* 详尽的细节	Unit 1
controller *n.* 管理员	Unit 8	electrode *n.* 焊条	Unit 6
corroded *adj.* 腐蚀的	Unit 9	electrolytic *adj.* 电解的	Unit 4
corrosion *n.* 腐蚀	Unit 9	electromechanical *adj.* 电动机械的	Unit 3
cost *n.* 损失	Unit 8	elevation *n.* 海拔	Unit 7
counter-currently *adv.* 逆流地	Unit 5	eliminate *v.* 除去	Unit 4
coupon *n.* 取样管,试样棒	Unit 4	elixir *n.* 万灵丹	Unit 8
covering *n.* 药皮	Unit 6	emergency *n.* 突发事故	Unit 9
crack *n.* 裂缝	Unit 4	emplace *v.* 安放,安置	Unit 3
crane *n.* 起重机	Unit 3	employer *n.* 业主	Unit 7
crawler *n.* 履带牵引装置	Unit 3	emulsifier *n.* 乳化剂	Unit 5
criterion *n.* 判断准则	Unit 8	enforce *v.* 执行	Unit 7
culvert *n.* 阴沟	Unit 7	engine *n.* 发动机	Unit 7
curvature *n.* 弯曲;曲率	Unit 3	erosion *n.* 侵蚀,腐蚀	Unit 8
cyanide *n.* 氰化物	Unit 10	estimate *v./n.* 估计	Unit 1
damp *v.* 受潮	Unit 6	evaporable *adj.* 易蒸发性的, 蒸发性的	Unit 10
debris *n.* 杂质瓦砾	Unit 7	excavation *n.* 开挖	Unit 2
decrease *v./n.* 减少	Unit 6	expansion *n.* 扩张	Unit 6
deformation *n.* 变形	Unit 3	exploration *n.* 勘探	Unit 1
dehydration *n.* 脱水	Unit 5	explosive *n.* 炸药	Unit 7
dehydrator *n.* 脱水器	Unit 5	extruder *n.* 挤压机	Unit 4
dent *v./n.* 凹下,凹进	Unit 3	extrusion *n.* 挤出	Unit 4
derrick *n.* 动臂起重机	Unit 3	factor *n.* 因素	Unit 6
describe *v.* 描述	Unit 6	FCAW 自保护药芯焊丝半自动焊	Unit 6
desiccant *n.* 干燥剂	Unit 5	felt *n.* 毡,毡制品	Unit 10
detailed *adj.* 详细的	Unit 7	filter *n./v.* 过滤,过滤器	Unit 9

filth *n.* 污物	Unit 10	hydrology *n.* 水文	Unit 1
filtration *n.* 过滤,筛选	Unit 10	imparted *adj.* 给予的,授予的	Unit 4
fit-ups *n.* 临时舞台	Unit 3	implement *n.* 工具,手段	Unit 8
fitting *n.* 配件	Unit 4	implementation *n.* 实施	Unit 7
flammable *adj.* 易燃的,可燃性的	Unit 10	indemnify *n.* 赔偿,保障	Unit 8
flotsam *n.* 废料,零碎物	Unit 3	inflammable *adj.* 易燃的	Unit 4
flux *n.* 助熔剂	Unit 6	inhibitor *n.* 抑制剂	Unit 4
folded *adj.* 折叠式	Unit 9	inspect *n.* 检查	Unit 8
foreman *n.* 工长	Unit 8	inspection *n.* 检测	Unit 9
forklift *n.* 铲车	Unit 4	inspector *n.* 检查员	Unit 7
formulas *n.* 公式,规则	Unit 1	install *v.* 安装	Unit 7
fort *n.* 要点	Unit 8	insulate *v.* 使绝缘,隔离	Unit 6
fractionate *v.* 精馏	Unit 1	insurance *n.* 保险	Unit 8
fume *n.* 烟尘	Unit 6	intermittent *adj.* 间歇的	Unit 6
function *n.* 作用	Unit 6	interruption *n.* 中断	Unit 6
fusion *n.* 熔合,熔接	Unit 6	investigation *n.* 调查	Unit 1
galvanic *adj.* 电流的,(电池)电流的	Unit 4	jack *n.* 千斤顶	Unit 3
gasifier *n.* 汽化器	Unit 9	join *n.* 接合点	Unit 6
gathering *n.* 集油(气)管网	Unit 1	joint *n.* 连接处,接缝	Unit 6
geographical *adj.* 地理学的,地理的	Unit 5	liable *adj.* 有责任的	Unit 8
grade *v./n.* 平整	Unit 2	line-up *n.* 对口	Unit 2
granular *adj.* 由小粒而成的,粒状的	Unit 5	loess *n.* (地理)黄土	Unit 8
graphitized *adj.* 石墨化的	Unit 4	longitudinal *adj.* 纵向的	Unit 7
gravel *n.* 碎石,沙石	Unit 8	lower-in *v.* 吊管下沟	Unit 2
grease *n.* 油脂	Unit 4	maintenance *n.* 维修	Unit 10
grid *n.* 电网	Unit 1	malfunction *n.* 故障	Unit 5
grip *n.* 把手,柄	Unit 3	malleable *adj.* 有延展性的,可锻的	Unit 3
grounding *n.* 接地	Unit 10	manual *adj.* 手工的	Unit 7
grout *v.* 用薄泥浆填塞	Unit 3	manually *adv.* 用手操作地	Unit 5
GTAW 钨极氩弧焊	Unit 6	maximum *adj.* 最大极限的	Unit 3
guarantee *v./n.* 保障	Unit 9	mechanized *adj.* 机械的	Unit 7
guide *v.* 导入	Unit 8	medium *n.* 介质,手段	Unit 9
hacksaw *n.* 钢锯	Unit 9	membrane *n.* 隔膜,隔板	Unit 3
hammer *n.* 手锤	Unit 9	mercaptan *n.* 硫醇	Unit 5
hazardous *adj.* 危险的	Unit 7	mercury *n.* 水银,汞	Unit 10
heater-treater *n.* 加热处理器	Unit 5	metallic *adj.* 金属(性)的	Unit 10
helium *n.* 氦	Unit 5	meter *vt.* 用表测量[计量,记录]; 计量[定量]供给	Unit 5
helmet *n.* 安全帽	Unit 7		
hobnail *n.* 平头钉	Unit 10	methane *n.* 甲烷	Unit 1
hoist *v.* 起重,提升,吊起	Unit 3	microbiological *adj.* 微生物学的	Unit 4
horizontal *adj.* 水平的	Unit 5	millesimal *n.* 千分之一	Unit 10
HSE 建康,安全,环保	Unit 7	molecule *n.* 分子,小粒	Unit 10
hudro-testing *n.* 试压	Unit 2	monitor *n.* 监测器	Unit 7
hydrate *n.* 水合物	Unit 5	monitor *v.* 检查	Unit 7
hydrocarbon *n.* 烃,碳氢化合物	Unit 1	monitoring *n.* 监视,控制,监测,追踪	Unit 5

mount *v.* 安装	Unit 3	power *n.* 电源	Unit 6
nest *v.* 使套入	Unit 3	precaution *n.* 预防,警惕	Unit 3
nipple *n.* 短节	Unit 9	prefabrication *n.* 配件预制	Unit 3
nitrogen *n.* 氮	Unit 1	premises *n.* (法律)前述事项	Unit 8
notification *n.* 通知	Unit 7	preservation *n.* 保护,维护	Unit 1
noxious *adj.* 有毒的	Unit 4	primed *adj.* 涂底漆的	Unit 4
nylon *n.* 尼龙	Unit 3	process *n.* 工序,工艺	Unit 6
offshore *adj.* 海上的	Unit 1	profile *n.* 外形	Unit 7
ohm *n.* 欧姆(电阻单位)	Unit 10	project *n.* 工程	Unit 7
onshore *adj.* 陆上的	Unit 1	provision *n.* 条文	Unit 8
operate *v.* 操作,执行	Unit 8	psi *n.* 磅	Unit 1
optimize *v.* 尽量有效地利用	Unit 8	pulse *n.* 脉搏,脉的一次跳动	Unit 8
Orinoco *n.* 奥里诺科河(南美洲北部)	Unit 2	purification *n.* 净化	Unit 5
oxidation-deteriorating *adj.* 氧化恶化的	Unit 4	PVC 聚氯乙烯	Unit 4
oxyacetylene *n.* 氧乙炔气	Unit 6	QHSE 质量、健康、安全、环境	Unit 7
padded *adj.* 填补的	Unit 3	qualified *adj.* 合格的	Unit 8
paraffin *n.* 石蜡	Unit 5	quality *n.* 质量	Unit 7
parameter *n.* 参数	Unit 7	quantity *n.* 数量	Unit 7
particle *n.* 粒子,微粒	Unit 5	radioactivity *n.* 放射性	Unit 10
pass *n.* 焊道	Unit 7	recruitment *n.* 休养	Unit 8
pathogen *n.* 微生物,病原体	Unit 10	refurbishment *n.* 整修	Unit 10
payment *n.* 支付	Unit 7	regulation *n.* 法规	Unit 8
peel *v.* 剥皮	Unit 4	rehabilitation *n.* 治疗,改造	Unit 9
penalty *n.* 惩罚	Unit 8	reinforce *v.* 加强	Unit 8
peril *n.* 隐患	Unit 10	reinforcement *n.* 加固材料	Unit 2
permafrost *n.* 永久冻结带	Unit 2	remedy *n./v.* 补救	Unit 9
permeability *n.* 渗透性	Unit 4	reservoir *n.* 油藏	Unit 2
phenomenon *n.* 现象	Unit 7	resilient *adj.* 有回弹力的	Unit 4
pickup *n.* 小型轻便货车	Unit 3	respiratory *adj.* 呼吸的	Unit 10
pig *n.* 清管器	Unit 9	respond *v.* 回复	Unit 7
pin *n.* 钉,栓,销	Unit 3	retain *v.* 保持,保留	Unit 5
pipeline *n.* 管道	Unit 9	reusable *adj.* 可重新使用的	Unit 9
pitting *n.* 蚀损斑	Unit 4	right-of-way *n.* 道路用地,施工带	Unit 3
plastify *v.* 热塑化	Unit 4	rivet *n.* 铆钉	Unit 6
plateaus *n.* 高原(pl. plateaux)	Unit 8	rooter *n.* 犁地机	Unit 2
pliable *adj.* 柔软的	Unit 3	roughness *n.* 粗糙度	Unit 1
pliers *n.* 扁嘴钳	Unit 9	rust *n.* 铁锈	Unit 10
PM 项目管理	Unit 7	sandblast *v./n.* 喷砂	Unit 4
poisonous *adj.* 有毒的	Unit 6	saponification *n.* 皂化	Unit 4
polarity *n.* 极性	Unit 6	saturate *v.* 浸透;使饱和	Unit 5
pollutant *n.* 污染物质	Unit 8	scaffolds *n.* 脚手架	Unit 3
polyethylene *n.* 聚乙烯	Unit 4	scaling *n.* 水垢形成	Unit 5
polypropylene *n.* 聚丙烯	Unit 4	schedule *v./n.* 安排	Unit 7
Polyurethane-Tar *n.* 聚亚安酯焦油	Unit 4	seam *n.* 焊缝	Unit 7
populous *adj.* 人口多的,人口稠密的	Unit 10	seepage *n.* 渗流	Unit 5

segment *n.* 部分,这里指管道	Unit 1	sustain *v.* 维持	Unit 6
separator *n.* 分离器	Unit 5	tally *n.* 记账;标签	Unit 3
shell *n.* 罐壁	Unit 9	Tanana *n.* 塔那那利佛	Unit 2
shut-down *n.* 停输	Unit 9	tarpaulins *n.* 防水油布	Unit 3
Siberia *n.* 西伯利亚	Unit 2	technician *n.* 技术员	Unit 8
sideboom *n.* 履带式起重机	Unit 3	tee *n.* 三通	Unit 9
skids *n.* 枕木,垫木	Unit 3	temporary *adj.* 临时的	Unit 7
slag *n.* 矿渣,炉渣	Unit 10	tendency *n.* 趋势	Unit 6
sling *n.* 钩悬带,吊索	Unit 3	terminal *n.* 终点站,终端	Unit 5
slowslope *n.* 缓坡	Unit 1	terrain *n.* 地带,地域	Unit 8
SMAW 焊条电弧焊	Unit 6	thermal *adj.* 热的	Unit 6
sober *n.* 混合器,萃取器	Unit 5	thermometer *n.* 温度计	Unit 10
socket *n.* 套筒扳手	Unit 9	tie-down *n.* 系住,拴住	Unit 3
soldering *n.* 软钎焊	Unit 6	tier *n.* 列,行,排,层	Unit 3
solidify *v.* (使)凝固	Unit 4	tong *n.* 钳子,夹具	Unit 3
sophisticated *adj.* 复杂的	Unit 1	top *n.* 罐顶	Unit 9
sorber *n.* 混合器,萃取器	Unit 5	topsoil *n.* 表层土	Unit 7
spatter *v.* 飞溅	Unit 7	torch *n.* 焊炬	Unit 6
specialize *v.* 专攻	Unit 7	tow *v.* 拖	Unit 3
specification *n.* 规格	Unit 7	toxic *adj.* 有毒的	Unit 10
sphere *n.* 橡胶球	Unit 9	toxicity *n.* 毒性	Unit 10
spherical *adj.* 球形的	Unit 5	trailer *n.* 拖车	Unit 3
spray *v.* 喷射	Unit 4	transmission *n.* 传送;输油(气)干线管道	Unit 1
spur *n.* 铁路支线,地方铁路	Unit 3	trench *n.* 沟	Unit 7
stability *n.* 稳定性	Unit 7	trial *n.* 试车	Unit 3
stainless *adj.* 不锈的	Unit 6	uncovering *n.* 开挖	Unit 4
stake *v.* 用木桩支撑	Unit 7	utilize *v.* 利用	Unit 4
static *adj.* 静态的,静力的	Unit 10	utmost *adj.* 最高的	Unit 8
stipulated *adj.* 规定的	Unit 1	*v.* 滑向一侧	Unit 3
stockpile *n.* 仓库	Unit 3	valve *n.* 阀门	Unit 10
stopple *v.* 封堵	Unit 9	vaporization *n.* 蒸发	Unit 1
stretcher *n.* 担架	Unit 8	Venezuela *n.* 委内瑞拉	Unit 2
stub *n.* 残片	Unit 7	vertical *adj.* 垂直的,直立的	Unit 3
sub-structure *n.* 下部(底部,基底)结构	Unit 3	vibration *n.* 振动	Unit 10
subcontract *n.* 续签合同	Unit 8	vigilant *adj.* 警惕的	Unit 4
subsidiary *n.* 附属人员	Unit 8	volume *n.* 体积,量	Unit 5
suction *n.* 抽吸	Unit 9	wagon *n.* 货车	Unit 3
sulfur *n.* 硫	Unit 5	welding *n.* 焊接	Unit 2
sundries *n.* 杂物	Unit 4	WEPP 西气东输工程	Unit 7
supervision *n.* 监理	Unit 7	winch *n.* 绞车	Unit 3
supervisor *n.* 检查员	Unit 8	workaround *n.* 工作区	Unit 10
supply *v.* 提供	Unit 7	wrap *n./v.* 缠绕	Unit 4
survey *v./n.* 调查	Unit 6	wrench *n.* 套筒扳手	Unit 9
suspension *n.* 悬挂式	Unit 9		

Phrases

adjustable wrench 活动扳手 Unit 9	crude trunk lines 原油干线 Unit 1
aging of heating coils 罐内加热盘管老化 Unit 10	CST Headquarters Office 工程监理总部 Unit 7
air bubble 气泡 Unit 4	cut off 切断 Unit 7
air compressor 空压机 Unit 9	data acquisition 数据采集 Unit 1
air strainer 空气过滤器 Unit 8	digestive system 消化系统 Unit 10
air-isolating layer 空气隔绝层 Unit 4	discharging rod 避雷针 Unit 8
allergic rhinitis 过敏鼻炎 Unit 8	disposable devices 一次性使用器具 Unit 8
anchor bolts 地脚螺栓 Unit 8	distribution terminals 分配油库 Unit 1
axial seam 轴向接缝 Unit 4	draining standard 排放标准 Unit 9
barrel type 桶式 Unit 9	drill frame 钻架 Unit 2
be attributed to 归因于 Unit 4	dropping boom 掉臂 Unit 8
be injected into 注入 Unit 9	dust catcher n. 除尘器 Unit 10
bottom plate 罐底板 Unit 9	electromagnetic radiation 电磁波辐射 Unit 10
brake device 刹车装置 Unit 3	emery cloth 金刚砂布 Unit 4
brake lining 制动衬面 Unit 3	epoxy resin 环氧树脂 Unit 4
breaking rope 断绳 Unit 8	erect temporary fences 设置临时墙 Unit 2
buffer zone 缓冲地带 Unit 8	erection work 安装工作 Unit 1
butt weld 对焊 Unit 6	ethylene perchloride 过氯乙烯 Unit 4
carbon dioxide 二氧化碳 Unit 1	Experience is the best teacher 实践出真知 Unit 9
cast iron pipe 生铁管 Unit 4	feasibility study 可行性研究 Unit 1
cathodic protection 阴极保护 Unit 1	ferrous metal 黑色金属 Unit 4
cementing material 胶结料 Unit 4	flammable gas 可燃性气体 Unit 9
centrifugal compressor 离心式压缩机 Unit 7	flow diagram 流程图 Unit 7
circulating (cycling) system 循环系统 Unit 9	flow line 出油(采气)管道 Unit 1
cleaning pig 清管器 Unit 4	flow meter n. 流量计 Unit 10
coal-tar enamel 煤焦油搪瓷 Unit 4	foam plastics 泡沫塑料 Unit 4
compliance with 遵照……行事 Unit 10	foul odor 恶臭 Unit 10
compressed air 压缩空气 Unit 4	fusion welding 熔接 Unit 6
condensed wax 结蜡 Unit 9	gas monitoring and oil/water separating system 气体检测及油水分离系统 Unit 9
Construction Law of People's Republic of China 《中华人民共和国建筑法》 Unit 8	gun barrel 沉淀罐,油水分离器 Unit 5
construction superintendent 工地主任 Unit 8	hand vice 手钳 Unit 9
controller staff member 管理员 Unit 8	heat exchanger 换热器 Unit 9
CPR=cardiopulmonary resuscitation 【医】心肺复苏法 Unit 8	heat shrinkable sleeve (tape) 热收缩带 Unit 4
	hook block 吊钩 Unit 8
crude oil 原油 Unit 5	hook spanner 钩扳手 Unit 9

hot bitumen 热沥青	Unit 2
hot-tapping and plugging 带压开孔、封堵	Unit 9
hydrogen sulfide 硫化氢	Unit 1
hydrologic geology 水文地质	Unit 1
idle time 停机[停歇,故障,中断运转]时间	Unit 1
impeded drainage 排水管线不畅	Unit 10
in compliance with 遵照……行事	Unit 10
in that case 既然那样	Unit 3
interior angle 内角	Unit 3
iron scrap 铁屑	Unit 10
kraft paper 牛皮纸	Unit 2
Laugh, and grow fat 心宽体胖	Unit 8
leak rate of the gasket-type seal point 静密封点泄漏率	Unit 10
lease automatic custody transfer 井区自动转输站	Unit 5
lease tank 油矿油罐	Unit 5
legal acquisition 合法用地	Unit 2
liquid nitrogen 液氮	Unit 9
loop seam 环向接缝	Unit 4
mineral area 矿区	Unit 1
mobile slewing crane 悬臂汽车吊	Unit 3
open end wrench 开口扳手	Unit 9
padding machine 垫土机	Unit 2
petrochemical plant 石油化工厂	Unit 1
physical property 物质性	Unit 9
pipe wrench 管扳手	Unit 9
polystyrene foam plastic 聚苯乙烯泡沫塑料	Unit 4
pressure gauge 压力表	Unit 10
pressure welding 压接	Unit 6
primary design 初步设计	Unit 1
processing plant 处理站	Unit 1
products pipeline 成品油管线	Unit 1
project manager 项目经理	Unit 7
ratchet wrench 棘轮扳手	Unit 9
reference materials 参考资料	Unit 7
repair under pressure 带压抢修	Unit 9
repair worker 维修工	Unit 9
reverse emulsion 水包油型乳液	Unit 5
right-of-way preparations 施工带准备	Unit 2
rotating ring hub assembly 回转环形毂盘部件	Unit 6
safety coordinator 安全协调员	Unit 8
Safety First 安全第一	Unit 7
safety helmet 安全帽	Unit 8
safety net 安全网	Unit 8
Safety Production Law of People's Republic of China《中华人民共和国安全生产法》	Unit 8
safety valve 安全阀	Unit 10
sanitary garbage 生活垃圾	Unit 10
screw driver 螺丝刀	Unit 9
see to 查看	Unit 3
seismic shocks 地震	Unit 2
self-act pressure regulator 自力式压力调节器	Unit 10
service lead assembly 服务线组件	Unit 6
shaft coupling 联轴器	Unit 3
shop drawing reconnaissance 施工图勘察	Unit 1
sideboom tractor 履带式吊管机	Unit 2
spherical pig trap 清管球收发筒	Unit 10
spot welding 点焊	Unit 6
spray gun 喷漆枪	Unit 4
spread working 综合施工	Unit 2
spreader bar 平压机	Unit 3
storage tank 储油罐	Unit 5
stray current 杂散电流	Unit 4
stringing pipe 布管	Unit 2
suspended matters 悬浮物	Unit 9
tank washing 油罐清洗	Unit 9
tar-like substance 焦油状物质	Unit 5
the extraction and suction system 抽吸系统	Unit 9
thermal fusion 熔化,熔解	Unit 4
thermal insulating layer 保温隔热层	Unit 4
to ease the itching and burning 止痒,减轻灼伤	Unit 8
to repair over again 返修	Unit 9
unidirectional fluid transportation 单向流体运输	Unit 1
uninterrupted operation 不间断运转	Unit 1
vaulted tank 拱顶罐	Unit 5
vaulted tanks 拱顶罐	Unit 5
vertical adjust 垂直调整	Unit 6
water leg 水夹套,水涨落速度装置	Unit 5
water strainer 滤水器	Unit 8
water vapor 水汽	Unit 5
weld ability 焊接性	Unit 6
weld joint 焊接接头	Unit 4
welding process 焊接工艺	Unit 6

welding sequence 焊接顺序	Unit 6	wheeled and tracked equipment 轮式和履带式设备	Unit 2
welding speed 焊接速度	Unit 6	wire rope 钢丝绳	Unit 3
welding technology 焊接技术	Unit 6	wiring box 配线盒	Unit 3
West-East Gas Pipeline Project 西气东输项目	Unit 8	work schedule 工作计划	Unit 8

参 考 书 目

1. 康勇编. *An English Course for the Petroleum Industry* 石油科技英语. 北京：石油工业出版社, 2005.
2. 朱芳冰, 谢从娇编. 石油工程专业英语. 武汉：中国地质大学出版社, 2005.
3. 冯叔初编. 石油储运英语教程. 北京：石油大学出版社, 1996.
4. 赵亮编. *Practical Terminology for Petroleum Pipeline* 石油管道实用英语. 中国石油天然气管道局, 2005.
5. 杨鑫南编. PRESENT-DAY AMERICAN ENGLISH DIALOGUES 当代美国英语会话. 北京：外语教学与研究出版社, 1989.
6. 李扬, 李沂编. *A Guide to U.S.A.* 赴美英语指南. 北京：外语教学与研究出版社, 1988.
7. （美）Ruth Pao-yu Li 编. 乔叟, 钟怡译. *AMERICAN TALK* 美语通用会话. 北京：外语教学与研究出版社, 1990.
8. 冯叔初编. 石油储运英语教程. 北京：石油大学出版社.
9. 唐江华, 冯春艳编. 天然气管道输送概论. 石油天然气管道职教中心.
10. 唐秀岐, 李姝编. *Oil & Gas Pipeline Technology*. 河北石油职业技术学院.
11. 康勇编著. 石油科技英语基础教程. 北京：石油工业出版社.